Santa Claus

COLLECTION

Santa Claus

COLLECTION

Volume 6
Meredith® Books
Des Moines, Iowa

The Magic of Santa Claus

The spirit of Christmas is upon us and what fun it is to celebrate with the love of Santa in our hearts. In this book you'll find the magic of Santa on every page. You'll feel his timelessness as you read stories about the colorful history that surrounds him. You'll chuckle when you see the collectibles and memorabilia that forever convey his image. You'll be impressed by the stunning collections that celebrate his uniqueness. You'll be amazed by the artistic talents of the craftspeople who create his likeness from wood, fabric, clay, and paint. And you'll even want to create some of your own magic as you see the clever Santa crafts and delicious sweet treats that you can make yourself.

So curl up in your favorite chair, reach for a cup of hot chocolate, and get ready to smile as you enjoy this book filled with the magic of the jolly old elf himself—Santa Claus!

Merry Christmas!

Opposite: *Santas made of clay, wood, resin, and fiber portray his warm appeal.*
Right: *Wood blocks in a wagon spell out Santa's name.*

Table of Contents

Opposite: *Inspired by Santas of the past, this group of Santas by Leo and Marilyn Smith* includes Chip on Shoulder, *some Belsnickles, and* Regal Santa.

LASTING LEGENDS

Wonderful legends of St. Nicholas and the historical presence of a child-loving gift giver evolved to give us Santa Claus— a generous spirit who brings presents to the world's children every Christmas.

A piece from Barbara Kissinger's collection shows the Woolson Spice Company's logo.

AND A HAPPY NEW YEAR

WISHES YOU A MERRY CHRISTMAS

The World's Greatest Traveler
Recommends

Interwoven
REG. U.S. PAT. OFF.

Socks for Christmas

Santa Sells in America

SANTA'S IMAGE MEANS A GREAT DEAL TO ALL WHO LOVE HIM,
AND SAVVY MARKETERS HAVE MADE USE OF THIS JOLLY OLD ELF.

There is no doubt about it. Santa Claus is a natural salesman. Who can resist the charms of the "right jolly old elf"?

Santa has been called on to promote many products during the holiday season throughout the last 140 years, from soap to oatmeal and from cigarettes to Coca-Cola. His sure-sell image had some help over the years from improved printing processes and a few superior 19th- and 20th-century illustrators who perfected his friendly spirit.

The earliest images of Santa in America began with author Washington Irving. Irving had written his book *Diedrich Knickerbocker's History of New York* in 1809 and its revision in 1812. The author's satire on life in early New York mentions St. Nicholas more than 20 times, describing him as an old Dutchman. In discussing the figurehead of St. Nicholas on the ship *Goede Vrouw,* Irving characterized it as "a goodly image of St. Nicholas, equipped with a low, broad-brimmed hat, huge pair of Flemish trunk hose and a pipe that reached to the end of the bowsprit."

The image of Santa Claus was further reinforced in 1822, when Clement C. Moore wrote his famous poem, "The Night Before Christmas," also known as "A Visit From St. Nicholas," for his own children. A number of differing paintings illustrated the poem as Santa's image evolved.

In 1837 James K. Paulding, Irving's brother-in-law, wrote of St. Nicholas, "the little rascal had on a three-cornered hat, decked with old gold lace, a blue Dutch sort of short pea jacket, red waistcoat, breeks (breeches) of the same colour, yellow stockings, and thick-soled shoes, ornamented with a pair of skates."

During this time St. Nicholas was also called St. Claus. Eventually that turned into Santa Claus, derived from the Dutch name Sinterklaas.

While advertising in general began in the 17th century with shop signs, Santa's foray into the field started in the 19th century, when newspapers began printing a picture of Santa alongside an ad in the classified section shortly before Christmas.

During the time of the Civil War in the early 1860s, political cartoonist Thomas Nast started drawing Santa

Opposite: *The Interwoven Sock Company used Santa to sell the idea of giving socks for Christmas.*

Written by Barbara Hallman Kissinger ✦ *Photographs by Andy Lyons*

Claus for *Harper's Weekly*. Nast envisioned him as a relative of his German homeland's Pelznickel, the fur-clad St. Nicholas. The artist showed Santa at the front lines delivering packages to the soldiers. He wore a Stars and Stripes uniform on the cover of *Harper's Weekly* in January 1863.

Santa's image was enhanced by color printing, or chromolithography, which was improving in the last half of the 19th century. The process began in 1837 when Godefroy Engelmann patented litho color printing, or lithography in color imitating painting.

Lithography involved a mechanical graphic process in which the printing and nonprinting areas of the plate were all at the same level. This differed from the intaglio and relief processes, which involved cutting designs into the printing block. Chromolithography was a printed color lithograph of at least three colors. Louis Prang, called the father of American Christmas and greeting cards, used chromolithography.

In the 1880s trade cards, which advertised a product and the store where it was available, became popular. They were bright and colorful due to chromolithography, and people collected them. The Victorians liked to paste them into scrapbooks, a favorite pastime.

Often printers using chromolithography made and sold seasonal trade cards to merchants, printing each store's message on the front, back, or both sides of a card. Customers could pick up the cards in the shops.

Many companies, such as Boos and Holbrook, distributed beautiful trade cards of Santa. One of these cards, Santa getting out of a sleigh, is a die-cut card with part of its stock cut away to leave an irregular shape that emphasizes the figure.

The Woolson Spice Company of Toledo, Ohio used trade cards as premiums for their products, especially Lion Coffee. The company became well known for its topical, seasonal, and holiday trade cards. Woolson also was the first company to introduce new cards each year, making them collectible. The J.C. Ayer Company of Lowell, Massachusetts used Santa trade cards in the

1840s to successfully market its Cherry Pectoral, a medicinal product.

The chromolithography process created some of the first colorful magazine ads of the late 1800s, including ones for the Pears Soap Company. Since soap barely existed in 1875, the image of Santa and his clothes all tarnished with ashes and soot created demand for the soap. Slabs of soap stood upright at the end of a store counter, and customers told the grocer how much they wanted cut off for purchase.

By the 1870s publishers such as *Harper's Monthly, Atlantic Monthly, Scribner's, Century,* and the *North*

Opposite and below: *Individual stores stamped their own names on cards using Santa to sell their products. Santa was used to sell everything from socks to cigarettes,* below *and* right.

Above: *From coffee to toys, Santa's image made every product more appealing.*

American Review started their first advertising sections in the back of the magazines. Other publications— *Saturday Evening Post, Collier's* and *Woman's Home Companion*—also carried large amounts of advertising.

In the 1890s photoengraving was introduced, which permitted the reproduction of tones of light and dark (halftones), as well as multiple-plate colors. The new development produced pictures that looked like paintings instead of pen-and-ink sketches and were less expensive to produce. The colorful trade cards faded out of existence, but Santa continued to sell.

Santa's image introduced the notion of breakfast foods after the Civil War. Oatmeal came first, but it

Above: *This Santa advertising for F. A. O. Schwarz travels with a gift-laden goat.*

took a long time to cook, often having to simmer overnight. By 1890 it could be cooked in a double boiler for 90 minutes. The top four cereal companies were Post, Kellogg, Quaker, and Shredded Wheat (which later became Nabisco). Shredded Wheat linked its product to Santa in an early 1900s ad.

Smoking increased with wartime, and Santa in uniform was right there promoting Murad cigarettes during World War I. Early American cigarettes were mixed with aromatic Turkish tobaccos, and Murad was a strong advertiser. (See Santa on page 13.)

Santa continued making political statements during World War II, promoting Interwoven Socks in 1944. The cartoon-style ad showed the United States (Santa) conquering Germany (Hitler), Italy (Mussolini), and Japan (Hirohito).

During the first half of the 1900s, illustrators of magazine covers enjoyed great popularity with Santa's help. Richard Felton Outcault created the comic strips "The Yellow Kid" and "Buster Brown," which ran from 1902 to 1920 in the *New York Herald*. Outcault licensed the character of Buster Brown to the Brown Shoe Company, which introduced Buster Brown Shoes in 1904 at the St. Louis World's Fair. Santa promoted Buster Brown Stockings in a magazine ad in December that same year.

Illustrator Joseph Christian Leyendecker, known as J. C. Leyendecker, sold his first of more than 300 covers to the *Saturday Evening Post* in 1899. He created many magazine covers and ads with Santa, including one for Interwoven Socks' argyle line and another for Pan American Coffee in 1940.

One of America's most beloved illustrators, Norman Rockwell, was commissioned to do four Christmas cards before his 16th birthday in 1910. He created Santa scenes for many covers for the *Saturday Evening Post* and for other magazines and advertisers, such as Pepsi-Cola. An illustration of Santa with an astronaut helmet appeared on the cover of *Family Circle* magazine in 1967.

The best-known illustrated images of Santa Claus were developed at the creative hands of Haddon Sundblom for Coca-Cola. He began creating ads for Coke in 1924. He produced annual paintings of Santa from 1931 to 1964. Sundblom's first model for Santa was his friend Lou Prentice. After Prentice's death, Sundblom is said to have used his own image.

Hand-drawn illustrations gave way to photography and television by the last half of the 20th century. In new forms, Santa continues to sell items today.

The Legend of St. Nicholas

OUR PRESENT-DAY JOLLY SANTA CLAUS HAS HIS ROOTS
IN A VERY OLD AND PROFOUNDLY COMPLEX ST. NICHOLAS.

Right: *This tin
Dutch Sinterklaas
is painted with rich
jewel-tone colors.*
Opposite: *Sinterklaas
sits on his white horse—
the way of travel for
this Christmas legend.*

A genealogist looking into our modern Santa Claus must dig into roots buried deeply in pre-Christian winter festivals that celebrated the Roman god Saturn. Santa's Christian heritage, however, begins with St. Nicholas, born during the third century in the port village of Patera, in what is now Turkey.

Orphaned by an epidemic when he was a young boy, Nicholas was placed in a monastery by his uncle, a priest. Six years later he was ordained. Not many years after that, he was named the Bishop of Myra, a city near his hometown, and was called the Boy Bishop.

Nicholas used his whole inheritance to help the sick and the needy and became known for his generosity and his love for children.

Under the Roman Emperor Diocletian, who persecuted Christians for not worshipping him as a god, Nicholas suffered for his beliefs and was exiled and imprisoned. Nicholas likely spent about 10 years in prison before Diocletian's successor, Constantine, released the prisoners.

After his release Nicholas attended the Council of Nicaea in A.D. 325. He died December 6, A.D. 343. The anniversary of his death became a day of celebration, St. Nicholas Day, to honor his devotion to the young and innocent.

Written by Carol McGarvey ✦ *Photographs by Scott Little*

Vive St. Nicolas!

Over the years many legends of St. Nicholas' life were told. A famous one involves a poor man with three daughters. It was the custom at the time that a young girl's father had to provide a prospective husband with a dowry. Without dowries the daughters would have to be sold into slavery. The daughters decided that one of them should enter a brothel to earn dowries for her sisters. They drew lots, and the oldest daughter lost. When Nicholas learned of the family's desperate straits, he wanted to help anonymously.

On three nights in succession, while the townspeople slept, small bags of gold were left at the poor man's home. On one night, Nicholas dropped his gold down the chimney, where it landed in a stocking hung to dry. After three nights each girl had a dowry. And Christmas legends started to form.

Sometimes the story is told with gold balls instead of bags of gold. That is why three gold balls—sometimes interpreted as oranges—are one of the symbols of St. Nicholas, the gift giver.

This story and others led to his canonization by the Catholic Church in the ninth century, and he became known as the patron saint of children. He also was revered for his care of sailors. Many stories exist of his appearing during great storms to calm the waters and to save a ship in peril. Sailors carried word of his kind deeds far and wide, and many St. Nicholas chapels are dedicated in many seaports. Devotion to the saint led to the building of more than 2,000 churches bearing his name in Russia, Belgium, England, Italy, and the Netherlands.

In 1087 a group of Italian sailors stole Nicholas' remains from his tomb in Myra to protect them from pirates and took them to Bari, Italy. Numerous examples

Opposite: *Postcards from Barbara Kissinger's collection depicting St. Nicholas are from the early 1900s.* Left: *A figurine dressed in red velvet can be seen at the Pella, Iowa, Historical Society.*

Opposite: *St. Nicholas kindly offers the children toys from his sack.*
Far left: *Sinterklaus's helper, Bad Pete, put naughty children in his bag.*
Left: *St. Nicholas rides his white horse.*

of healing took place when his remains arrived in Italy. The people of Bari built a magnificent church in his honor and for his crypt. The shrine became a great pilgrimage center.

Stories about St. Nicholas and his popularity continued to grow throughout Europe, and the eve of his feast day, December 5, became an occasion for giving small gifts, such as fruits and nuts, in shoes, in stockings, on windowsills, or beside beds.

During the Protestant Reformation in the 16th century, however, Martin Luther decried the worship of saints. Giving gifts during a midwinter festival didn't die out, but rather moved to a different date, Christmas day.

In the place of St. Nicholas, another group of gift givers—more secularized in their approach—gained favor.

In Belgium and Spain the three Wise Men delivered gifts to children on the feast of the Epiphany. Children left straw for the Wise Men's camels, and, with any luck, there would be gifts the next morning.

Father Christmas in England and his counterpart in France, Père Noël, brought gifts for well-behaved children. Grandfather Frost was the gift bearer in Russia. After the Reformation in Germany, numerous figures became popular, from Pelze Nichol, or Pelznichol, a stern judge of behavior, to Christkind, an angelic messenger from Jesus. In the Netherlands, it was Sinterklaas. There were women as well, including La Befana in Italy and Babouschka in parts of Russia.

Dutch and English settlers enhanced the Christmas celebration in America. Father Christmas and St. Nicholas melded into one figure. The old name of St. Nicholas, Sinter Claes, became Santa Claus.

The contemporary Santa evolved from Clement C. Moore's "*Twas the Night Before Christmas*" poem, 19th century illustrations by Thomas Nast, and Haddon Sundblom's images that appeared in Coca-Cola advertising in the 1930s.

There's no question that the lore of St. Nicholas and Santa Claus is part myth with historical overtones. But don't tell that to children. To them, he's very real.

Sinterklaas: The Dutch St. Nicholas

Sinterklaas is the Dutch interpretation of St. Nicholas. When he arrives in a community of Dutch heritage, such as Pella, Iowa, the children know the Christmas season has begun. Pella hosts a Sinterklaas parade, and children dress in costumes as gingerbread men, snowmen, shepherds, angels, snowflakes, elves, wise men, Tiny Tim, drummer boys, and sugarplum fairies.

The community's traditional Dutch storefronts, Molengracht canal, and the tall Tulip Toren (tower) provide the perfect historical backdrop for the anticipated parade.

Sinterklaas is the patron saint of Amsterdam, and during the holidays he arrives by boat from Spain and sails through town wearing a red cloak and tall mitered hat. After the parade a Sinterklaas party is held at the beautifully restored Pella Opera House.

It is believed that Sinterklaas rides over rooftops listening at chimneys to check on children's behavior. By the fireplace children leave wooden shoes filled with carrots and hay for the horse. The Piets, Sinterklaas' helpers, exchange the feed for candies and small gifts.

Sinterklaas gives good children Dutch letters and chocolate coins, while others may find sticks and coal in their shoes.

Besides the arrival of Sinterklaas, a Christmas Walk takes place at the Pella Historical Village and a Christmas Tour of Homes is sponsored by the Pella Garden Club.

Sinterklaas and his spirit endure in south central Iowa as well as other Dutch communities around the world.

A porcelain representation of Sinterklaas sits in front of a mirrored windmill in this European vignette.

TIMELESS MEMORABILIA

The Christmas season evokes
nostalgic feelings as we remember
past holidays. Who could
forget the legendary *Night Before
Christmas*, or childish tales
of Santa's elves, or selecting the
family Christmas tree?

Left: *These tiny stamps and Christmas seals from
the mid-1900s were collected for their charm and
never used.*

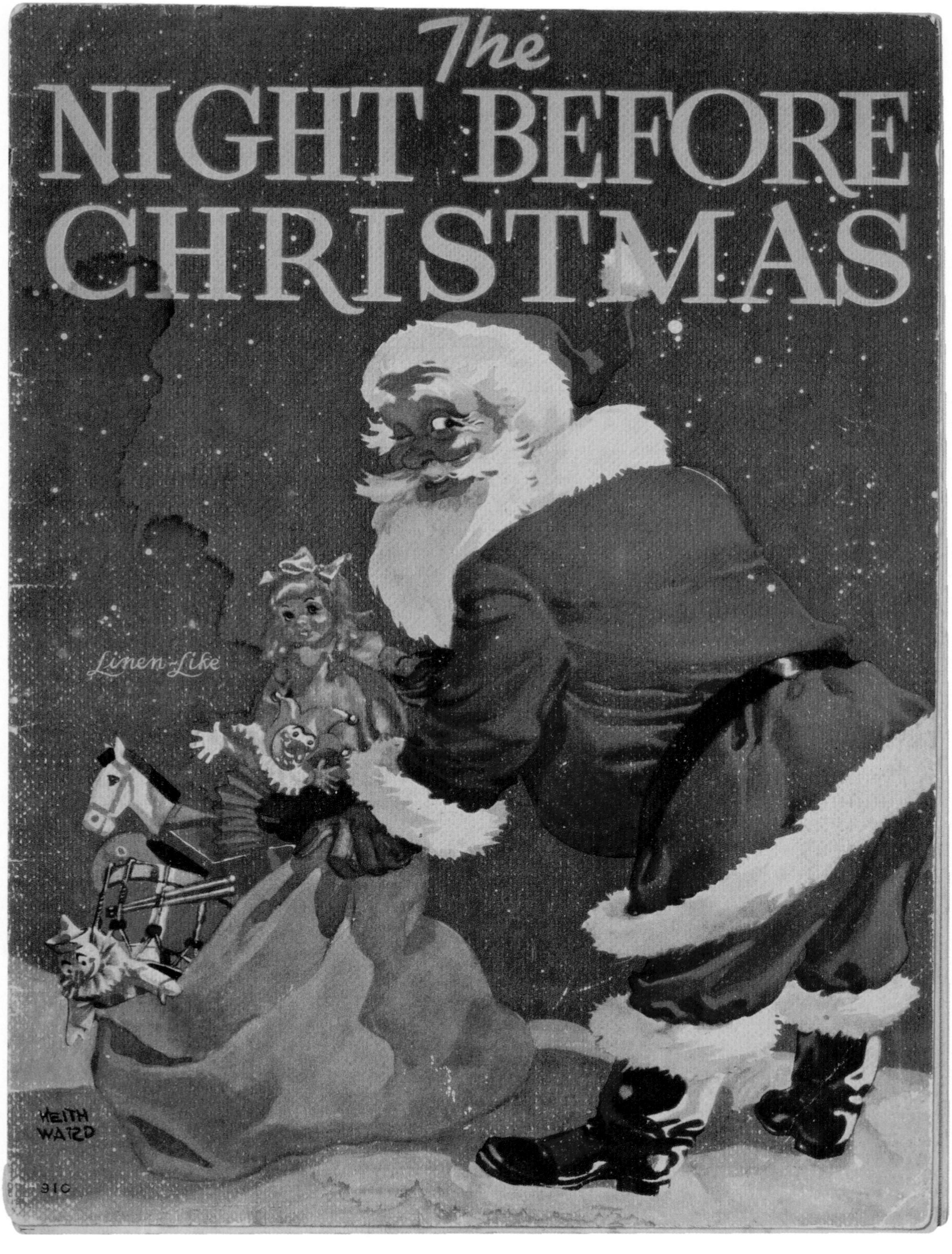
The
NIGHT BEFORE
CHRISTMAS
Linen-Like
KEITH
WARD
310

A Christmas Classic

THERE ARE MANY HOLIDAY BOOKS, BUT THE ALL-TIME FAVORITE, OF COURSE, IS *THE NIGHT BEFORE CHRISTMAS*, PENNED IN 1822 BY CLEMENT C. MOORE. IN PROSE THAT MADE IT EASY FOR YOUNG AND OLD ALIKE TO VISUALIZE SANTA'S JOURNEY, MOORE CREATED A HOLIDAY LEGACY.

The story goes that Moore wrote *The Night Before Christmas* first entitled, *A Visit From St. Nicholas,* on Christmas Eve in 1822. His family was on a sleigh ride home after a visit to Greenwich Village. The poem was published anonymously in the *Troy Sentinel* of New York on December 23, 1823.

Moore was a biblical scholar and taught Greek and Oriental literature in the Episcopal seminaries of New York City from 1821 to 1850. Some historians believe that Moore drew inspiration for the roly-poly St. Nick from the Dutchman who drove his sleigh that day. Others believe that the studious professor drew his mental picture from literary sources, such as Washington Irving's *Knickerbocker History,* written in 1809, and a Christmas poem called "The Children's Friend," written in 1821.

It is believed that Moore used the descriptions of the rotund and jolly Dutch burghers with their red cloaks, wide belts, and white beards to create his story. And while the poem he read had one reindeer, he added seven more. The poem combined customs of the Dutch references to St. Nicholas (Sinterklaas in Dutch).

Opposite: *Artist Keith Ward's interpretation of Santa Claus is a little less roly-poly in a 1935 book published by Whitman Publishing Company.* Above: *Whitman Publishing Company printed a 1938* The Night Before Christmas *book. Interior pages have a muted look.*

Written by Carol McGarvey ✦ *Photographs by Andy Lyons* ✦ *Books courtesy of Harry and Barbara Budd*

As dry leaves that before the
wild hurricane fly,
When they meet with an obstacle,
mount to the sky,
So up to the housetop
the coursers they flew
With a sleigh full of toys and
Saint Nicholas, too.
And then in a twinkling
I heard on the roof
The prancing and pawing
of each little hoof.
As I drew in my head and
was turning around,
Down the chimney Saint Nicholas
came with a bound.

He was dressed all in fur
from his head to his foot,
And his clothes were all tarnished
with ashes and soot.
A bundle of toys he had flung
on his back,
And he looked like a peddler just
opening his pack.
His eyes—how they twinkled!
His dimples—how merry!

Above: Sharon Banigan illustrated this 1953 book by Whitman Publishing Company. As with some other books in the 1950s, Santa's suit has a fuzzy texture. Below: A full-figured Santa graces the cover of this 1958 rendition, published by Merrill Publishing Company.

He wrote the poem as a gift to his six children. Even when others received it enthusiastically, he refused to have it published. However, a family member is said to have submitted it to the newspaper. Moore didn't acknowledge it until 15 years later. Because of that, speculation exists that Henry Livingston, Jr., a land surveyor and poet, actually composed the classic.

Over the many years that Barbara and Harry Budd of Ames, Iowa have added to their Santa collection of 4,500 pieces (see "All Through the House," *page 50*), Barbara has developed a side collection of 150 *Night Before Christmas* books. The Budds search flea markets, estate and garage sales, and shops to find books. Often it's the style of the illustrator that causes a sale, Barbara

Above: *Saalfield Publishing Company distributed this 1951 version, illustrated by Ethel Hays.* Below: *An early book with no date, published by M.S. Donohue & Company, touts itself as being "profusely illustrated." Inside pages are printed in black and white.*

says. A special book from 1938 commemorates the year of her birth. Artist Grandma Moses illustrated another, which was hard to find. Earlier versions from the 1920s and early 1900s are characterized by interesting drawings. One early book even claimed that it was "profusely illustrated." The books point out how Santa's appearance changed as his name evolved. Europeans

had depicted St. Nicholas as a tall, thin, stately figure. Americans Washington Irving and later Clement C. Moore created a picture of the "right jolly old elf" as a round figure with twinkling eyes and a white beard, wearing a bright red suit.

Barbara says Thomas Nast, an American cartoonist, and Haddon Sundblom, an illustrator for Coca-Cola,

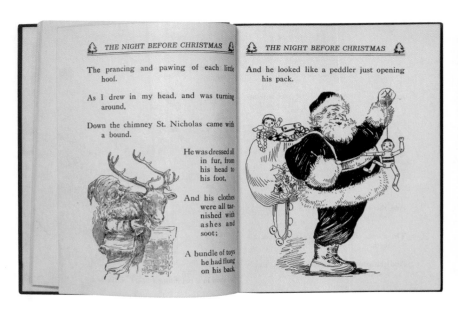

"Now, Dasher! Now, Dancer! Now, Prancer
and Vixen!
On, Comet! On, Cupid! On, Donner
and Blitzen!
To the top of the porch, to the top
of the wall!
Now, dash away! Dash away! Dash away, all!"
As dry leaves that before the wild hurricane fly
When they meet with an obstacle mount
to the sky,
So up to the housetop the coursers they flew
With a sleigh full of toys and
Saint Nicholas too.
And then in a twinkling I heard on the roof
The prancing and pawing
of each little hoof.
As I drew in my head and was turning around,
Down the chimney Saint Nicholas came
with a bound.

Above: *Santa's fuzzy suit, illustrated by Vivian Robbins for Whitman Publishing Company, is on the cover of this 1959 book.* Below: *An early undated book by Merrill Publishing Company features delicate illustrations.*

made that picture even more pronounced in their artistic creations.

Barbara has nearly 300 other books with holiday themes. One prized possession is a Dell Christmas comic book, which sold for 10 cents in 1953. She has several books with fuzzy covers, an earmark of the 1950s.

Another Christmas Tale

Barbara and Harry Budd collect other Santa Claus books as well as *The Night Before Christmas*. Here are some favorites:

Clockwise from above left: Polygraphic Company of America produced a ring-bound pop-up book, *Santa's Merry Carnival*, in 1955. Barbara Budd took several torn pages apart and painstakingly repaired them. *Kiddies' Christmas*, published in 1937 by Remick Music Corporation, combines coloring pages and sheet music for holiday songs. The Doehla Greeting Card Company published a wire-bound Santa storybook in 1950. *Below from left:* A Dell comic book, 10 cents when new, was published in 1953 by Western Printing Company. A 1907 songbook features music and lines for a Christmas cantata by Charles Gabriel. Fillmore Music House published it. The undated *Story Book for Christmas* features some Santa illustrations with scary faces, a precursor to jolly Santa drawings.

Santa's Elves

TINY DOLL-LIKE FIGURES OF ELVES AND SANTA WERE MADE
IN JAPAN FROM INEXPENSIVE MATERIALS IN THE MID-1900S. THESE
CHARMING COLLECTIBLES ARE THOUGHT TO BRING GOOD LUCK.

Written by Carol McGarvey ✦ *Photographs by Scott Little*

Santa Claus is the original multitasking head of his own little North Pole corporation. But even Santa admits that he needs help for the daunting production that takes place every Christmas Eve. Growing numbers of children around the world need toys and other gifts. Packing the sleigh alone takes hours. Who helps him? Elves, gnomes, and tomptes, that's who. They answer to various names but likely came on the scene in the pagan era in Scandinavia. It was believed that gnomes guarded homes against evil. While they were thought to be benevolent, it seems they could turn nasty when they were not treated well.

During the mid-1800s, when the celebration of Christmas grew in popularity as a midwinter festive season, Scandinavian writers told of elves and their role as fairy creatures who were full of mischief. At the same time, however, they were loyal helpers to Father Christmas, later known as Santa Claus. Artists of the era started incorporating the elves in their work.

The elves' homeland is considered to be Lapland, on the Finnish-Russian border. Their father is Gryla and their mother is Leppaludi. The number of elves

Opposite: *Santa becomes elf-like as he makes music and skis at the same time.* Right: *Santa's elves show up as decorations in a fun-loving holiday band. During the jam session, elves play trumpets, cymbals, and accordions. The center elf proudly holds a stocking.*

varies, depending on the source. Some say 13, while others believe there are 9 or 6. Their names vary too. Some of the old names are so long that they couldn't fit on the back of a T-shirt—Bjugnakraekir, Gattathefur, Ketkrokur, and Skyrgámur. Other books cite some later, shorter names—Barnid, Sjalfur, Redda, Sledda, Tifill, and Tutur. Still other sources offer some modern names—Bushy Evergreen, Shinny Upatree, Wunorse Openslae, and Alabster Snowball.

Their duties, of course, fit their purpose of spreading joy. Some make toys, while others keep the sleigh in working order, feed reindeer, make holiday treats with Mrs. Claus, and keep tabs on the all-important Naughty and Nice list. A legend tells that on January 6, the last day of Christmas, elves light torches and come down from their secret mountain hideaway to celebrate a job well done.

In the mid-1900s, right after World War II, countless holiday knickknacks were made in Japan. Usually made from inexpensive materials, these figures cost only a few cents. Christmas gnomes and Santas were among the tiny creations sent from overseas and purchased at dime stores. Now more than 50 years later, these tiny dolls are collectible, ranging in price from $10 to $40.

Maybe it is the tiny scale that makes these collectibles so charming, or perhaps it is the good luck that they promise to bring. Over time the phrase "Santa's elves" has taken on new meaning. It often is used to refer to people who do kind deeds at Christmas, volunteering to wrap gifts, preparing and serving food at shelters, and donating presents for children. Maybe these tiny helpers are just a reminder of that holiday spirit we all hope to have.

Right top: *This elf shares an endearing expression as he pauses holding a tiny tree.* Right: *Three elves form a happy trio.* Opposite: *Dime store papier-mâché houses were common decorations in the mid-1900s.*

Miniature Papier-Mâché Houses

Other tiny and inexpensive knickknacks came into the country in the mid-1900s, including charming papier-mâché houses. Made from folded cardboard and covered with glitter, these miniature homes often were sold as a set or village for 25 cents or less at dime stores.

Sometimes the windows in the house had tiny pieces of cellophane glued behind the opening or a small printed window pieced into the window frame. The houses varied in style from a typical cottage shape to a flat-roofed house. Occasionally the villages had churches or other buildings in the set. Oftentimes the doors could open and close. The house or building was glued to a flat piece of cardboard. Little bottlebrush-style trees were glued to the base and dusted with glitter to complete the setting.

Forever '50s!

THE 1950S GAVE US SANTAS AND IMAGES OF CHRISTMAS THAT WILL FOREVER MAKE US SMILE.

Looking back with perspective, the 1950s were fabulous, funky, and fun, especially at Christmastime.

If you had a real Christmas tree in your home, likely you didn't go to a tree farm to tag it and cut it. If you lived in town, no doubt your family carefully selected one from the long row of trees outside the grocery store. This was the drill—pick one, pull it from the stack, hold it with one hand, and pound its trunk several times on the sidewalk to get it to shake down.

Trees with a pronounced open spot were positioned with that part against the wall or facing a corner.

After decorating it at home with overly colorful ornaments, paper chains, and pinecones dipped in glue and glitter, the final step—putting on the icicles or silver tinsel—required an artistic flair. Mother always wanted the tinsel put on piece by piece, but little brother always threw it in clumps toward the top of the tree. At the end of the season, the goal was to retrieve as much tinsel as possible for next year, trying to arrange it over the cardboard so it could slide back into a long, narrow box. Impossible!

In many homes, however, it wasn't a green tree that took center stage. It was an artificial silver

Above: *Santa shapes form an interesting string of holiday lights. They were made in Japan.* Left: *A plastic Santa camera is a 1950s collectible.* Opposite: *A kindly Santa figurine shows a fatherly face.*

Written by Carol McGarvey ✦ *Photographs by Andy Lyons*

A group of Santa Clauses from the mid-1900s often decorated mantels, tables, and Christmas trees. Many were designed to hold candies in Santa's pack on his back.

aluminum tree. Standard lights were too hot for this type of tree, so to make it dramatically colorful, a lighted round disk attached with red, green, blue, and yellow sections was used. As the electric disk moved around, the various colors made the tree appear to glow. Today these trees are highly collectible, especially for retro or contemporary settings.

A number of holiday decorations from the 1950s were labeled "Made in Japan." At the time some consumers considered them a bit inferior in quality, but today they are sought after. Santa lights made of pipe cleaners fit that category.

Plastic this and plastic that were hits for the holidays. Santa and snowman figures were particularly prevalent. Santa was on skis or sitting in a sleigh pulled by white plastic reindeer. Some Santas and snowmen had open spots in packs on their backs to hold little candies or toys.

Wall decorations, such as plastic Santa faces, were popular for generating a bit of holiday magic inside the home or welcoming guests on the front door. Christmas seals were sent out as fund-raisers, and consumers decorated gift packages and greeting card envelopes with them to spread a bit of holiday cheer.

Holiday music was a festive mix—from "Blue Christmas" by Elvis Presley to the ever-growing hits of "White Christmas" by crooner Bing Crosby and "Rudolph the Red-Nosed Reindeer" by singing cowboy Gene Autry. Radio and vinyl records were the sources for listening.

During the decade, homes took on a new concept: television. While families remained loyal to their radio favorites of Fibber McGee and Molly and The Great

Gildersleeve, they also became hooked on *Wagon Train, Bonanza,* and *I Love Lucy.* Junior high girls rushed home from school to watch their favorite dancers and heartthrobs—Kenny Rossi, Arlene Sullivan, Pat Molittieri, and Eddie Kelly—on *American Bandstand.*

Not surprisingly the decade that spawned the hula hoop, the Frisbee, sweater twinsets, and poodle skirts celebrated the holidays in pretty cool ways too.

This faded felt stocking includes a scene of Santa on his Christmas Eve journey.

Christmas fabric items courtesy of Donna Chesnut

Santa often appeared on holiday fabrics in the mid-1900s. From below clockwise, *a printed tablecloth, a Santa and reindeer motif on a tree skirt, and a sweet Christmas hankie.*

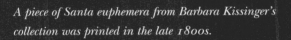

A piece of Santa euphemera from Barbara Kissinger's collection was printed in the late 1800s.

The message of Christmas is one of joy and giving. So it's not surprising that devoted collectors of Santas not only enjoy their treasures all year long, they also love sharing them with the rest of us.

DEVOTED COLLECTORS

The Faces of Santa

THIS PASSIONATE SANTA COLLECTOR HAS A REAL CONNECTION WITH EACH JOLLY OL' ELF SHE BRINGS HOME.

Aside from her grown sons, David and Evan, the men in Vicki Sivesind's life all seem to have the same initials—S.C. "I have always loved Santa Claus," says this avid collector.

After living in the Northeast part of the country for 12 years, Vicki was widowed suddenly when her sons were five and one. "If I was going to raise them alone, I decided I wanted to do it in my hometown around family and friends."

When she moved in 1987, she started going to craft shows and noticed a trend. "I found all these people who made wonderful Santas, and I just started collecting. I couldn't help myself." Vicki looks for distinct figures wherever she travels or shops.

How does she choose? It's all in the faces, she says. "I look for a face that is kind because that's what Santa Claus is all about. If there are several before me, I line them up and study them before selecting one. It's very

important." For that reason she has very few old-world-style Santa figures, because their faces are often quite stern.

"The eyes need to twinkle," insists the collector. "Santa's face must be friendly."

Vicki tells the story of one patriotic Santa wearing a quilted cloak. "He was made in October 2001, right after the tragedy of September 11. The pensive, worried look on his sculpted face just spoke to me. He did and does have a comforting presence that is very special."

Vicki enjoys collecting works of various artists. "I am so appreciative and in awe of what some of these artists

Above left: *This tender polymer clay face and fluffy fur beard appeal to Vicki.* Opposite: *Papier mâché, wood, paper pulp, and resin Santas show the different styles in hats, faces, and cloaks.*

Written by Carol McGarvey ✦ *Photographs by Andy Lyons*

create. I'm not artistic myself, but I love what they do, and I'm always amazed at the differences they bring to life." Vicki does, however, create counted cross-stitch and perforated paper Santas.

Sometimes the material of the Santas showcases the differences. She has Santas made from wood, paper pulp, bark, polymer clay, and resin and even some hand-painted on cowbells, horns, and ratchet toys.

SANTA SMILES EVERYWHERE

Vicki's large collection seems understated because of the way she has it arranged. In her family room she has smaller versions amassed on shelves of an open bookcase for emphasis. In her dining room a buffet is used for display. In the living room they fill a glass hutch and the top of a piano. "I tend to enjoy antiques and wood pieces, especially those from the Arts and Crafts era that can be used to enhance the Santa collection."

She also has an extensive collection of Santa-inspired jewelry—necklaces, pins, and earrings—and often has

Right: *Santa Claus is a focal point over the family room fireplace. Painted on a wood board, he came from a farmhouse in Massachusetts.* Opposite, clockwise from above left: *A wise-looking patriotic Santa with a friendly-face was fashioned by Jayne Frerichs an Illinois artist. Designer Denise Calla of House of Hatten styled the Santa character in a white cloak, carrying a holiday tree. Another patriotic Santa, with his pensive, worried face and quilted cloak, was fashioned by Jayne Frerichs right after the tragedy of September 11, 2001. The set of Santas were designed by two different artists— California artist Debbie Thibault fashioned the one on the left of papier-mâché. On the right is one made of paper pulp and signed A. Wobler.*

to wear several each day to wear them all during the holiday season.

Miniature Santas, with figures on golf tees, needle cases, and oyster shells, give another dimension to her collection. In addition she looks for interesting *Night Before Christmas* books, fascinating pop-up books, and holiday jigsaw puzzles. When she's not shopping in stores or at craft shows, she finds new inspiration on eBay on the Internet.

For the holidays Vicki puts up two Christmas trees. One holds ornaments she has given to her sons each year. The other is her tree and holds her personal collection of Santa ornaments.

Vicki, who is known as "the Santa lady" to many in her area, has a sign over her family room door that leads to an enclosed patio that says it all: "I Believe in Santa Claus." And you know that in her heart, she does.

Above: *An antique shelf holds some of Vicki's Santas from around the world.* Right: *A Scandinavian look is natural on this Santa. The carved texture on his mustache and beard brings dimension to the figure made in Decorah, Iowa, home of the Norwegian-American Museum.* Opposite: *This Santa came to Vicki's home by way of Montreal, Canada. He is hand-sculpted and wears a rich tapestry cloak. Besides packages he carries plum pudding.*

All Through the House

THIS GENEROUS COUPLE BRINGS JOY TO A COMMUNITY
BY OPENING UP THEIR HOME TO SHARE A LOVE OF SANTA
CLAUS AND HELP NEEDY CHILDREN AT THE SAME TIME.

Just like Santa Claus himself, Barbara and Harry Budd of Ames, Iowa carry the spirit of giving in their hearts. This is the fifth Christmas season they have opened their home to tours of their Santa collection—more than 4,500 pieces—with all proceeds going to a local program that serves children with emotional and behavioral disorders.

"We really have no idea how we gathered so much stuff," says Harry with amazement. "We're obviously completely out of control."

But it all started to make sense when a visitor suggested that sharing the collection to benefit children was a wonderful idea. "Certainly, Christmas is a religious holiday, but I think that Santa also embodies that giving, caring spirit without becoming too commercial," Harry insists.

He and Barbara have collected for many years. Their full-to-the-rafters 1915 foursquare-style home proves that. But they still keep their eyes open for the next treasure. They have ornaments, figures large and small, dishes, pot holders, puzzles, books, and toys in their huge collection.

The Budds, married for 45 years, have two sons and four grandchildren. Everyone in the extended family loves the Christmas items and continues to look out for more. When Barbara and Harry travel, they naturally seek new Santa interpretations. That's how they acquired a Santa made from a gourd in the South, a pottery Santa figure with delicate Queen Anne's lace glazed into the design, and a "banana Santa" made in a village in Kenya from a banana leaf.

The couple's home is a duster's nightmare. Breakfronts, buffets, and bookshelves are filled with Santa characters. They have rugs, prints, strings of

Opposite: *An antique trunk showcases a treasure trove of Santa-inspired pastimes, including a count-by-number game, a jump rope, a yo-yo, playing cards, trains, plastic toys, and books.* Left: *This plastic Santa from the 1950s holds an evergreen.*

Written by Carol McGarvey ✦ *Photographs by Andy Lyons*

Christmas Classic

On the landing of the steps leading to even more rooms filled with Santas, there are two large Santa heads—probably once used in store windows. This type of Santa is usually made of thin plastic.

lights, serving pieces, goblets, and enough mugs to serve the neighborhood. Porcelain music boxes play "Here Comes Santa Claus." Santa-trimmed tins and four gift givers form a fireplace screen.

Harry and Barbara also collect antique pieces, such as an old treadle sewing machine, a rolltop desk with lots of nooks and crannies, and an Underwood No. 3 manual typewriter. Of course a "Dear Santa" letter rests in the carriage. "We look for antiques that will make good props for some of the Santa items," explains Harry.

SANTAS EVERYWHERE

The Budds have allowed themselves a pair of comfy chairs and a TV in an upstairs bedroom. The rest of the room is devoted to Coca-Cola Santas—yes, they have a life-size one by Coke illustrator Haddon Sundblom—and a stack of 500- and 1,000-piece Christmas jigsaw puzzles. They have assembled most of them. Smaller holiday items include Pez dispensers, including some in German and Chinese packaging, and a handmade roly-poly Santa on a pull-cart. They even have a Santa shape made from a lobster buoy.

The dining room table is set with festive Fitz & Floyd china in the Santa's List pattern. Santa chair covers fit right in with holiday glassware, cheese picks, swizzle sticks, and a corkscrew with a Santa handle.

Separately Harry and Barbara say they have insisted on "no more Santas." Then one of them sees a

tempting figure at a flea market or garage sale, finding it hard to pass up another example of Santa's appeal. "I really enjoy a piece that's cheap and unique," Barbara explains. "Even if a piece is worn or bent, I can usually fix it with a little patience."

When she prepares a meal, Barbara is surrounded by Santa's charm in the kitchen. Shelves are filled with cookie cutters, molds, and recipe booklets. Staples are stored in clear canisters with red lids and Santa figures on the sides. Fortunately red is Barbara's favorite color, so it complements the festive look in the kitchen. She has a red stand mixer, a red blender, and a red toaster. Cabinets are painted a soft green.

When it was time to reupholster the sofa and settees in the living room, the couple chose dark burgundy to enhance the collection.

Santa Claus memorabilia comes in all sizes, with the tiniest being about one-half inch. The largest Santa possession of the Budds is the life-size Coke design. They have paid next to nothing for some pieces and dearly for a few special contemporary ones.

Opposite: *Santa even fills the kitchen with his image.*
Above left: *Harry and Barbara Budd sit among their thousands of Santas.* Above: *These items from the 1980s caught their attention. With the flick of a switch, the battery-run Santa drives a car that shimmies, lights flash, and eyes twinkle. Another Santa pushes a drum and clangs cymbals playing "Santa Claus Is Coming to Town."*

FOR THE CHILDREN

When they became part of the "elf network," the Budds teamed up with the city Jaycees to sponsor their home tour each year. Adults pay $3 to tour the collection, and children 12 and under enter free. All proceeds benefit Beloit Residential Treatment Center in Ames, a program of Lutheran Social Service of Iowa that helps children from 5 to 13. The Budds had nearly 700 visitors last year. They have welcomed guests from all over the United States.

Besides the tour the couple aims to provide books requested by children when they leave the Beloit home. They have gone searching for books as diverse as *The Sword and the Stone* to a parent-child cookbook.

As special as the whole Santa collection is, one framed piece faces the couple when they come down the stairs each morning. It is a thank-you letter signed by some of the children at the home:

"One hundred years from now, it will not matter what my bank account was, the sort of house I lived in, or the kind of car I drove, but the world may be different because I was important in the life of a child."

A framed piece of artwork made especially for Barbara and Harry holds a special place in their hearts.

A Christmas Classic

Many holiday books have been written, but the all-time favorite is *The Night Before Christmas*. Barbara has collected about 150 with that title. (See *pages 26–31*.) A special one from 1938 commemorates the year of her birth. Artist Grandma Moses illustrated another, which was hard to find. Versions from the 1920s and earlier are characterized by interesting drawings. One even touted that it was "profusely illustrated."

Barbara has about 300 other books with holiday themes. One from 1937, called *Kiddies' Christmas*, features an interesting mix of nine Christmas carols with sheet music and corresponding pictures to color. The original cost was 25 cents. Some of the songs include "Jingle Bells," "It Came Upon a Midnight Clear," and "Silent Night." Still other books feature thick textured paper, making it durable in little hands.

Barbara likes other musical pieces that feature Santa as well. One vintage Christmas record offers words to live by for good girls and boys:

1. Listen to Mommy and Daddy.
2. Mind your teacher.
3. Be neat and clean.
4. Go to bed early.
5. Be kind to animals.
6. Brush teeth twice a day.
7. Be careful crossing streets.
8. Don't be selfish.
9. Be courteous.
10. Go to church.

A timeworn Old Brunswick treadle sewing machine is set for making Christmas projects. The theme continues with the Santa pincushions and spools.

Around the World

COLORFUL HOLIDAY POSTCARDS FROM ALL AROUND THE
WORLD SHOW THE DIFFERENCES AND THE SIMILARITIES
IN THE EVOLUTION OF SANTA CLAUS.

Above: *Barbara Kissinger, dressed as Mrs. Claus, shows her
postcards.* Opposite: *Santa's at the top of the world as he is
featured in this collection of rare postcards.* Above right: *Father
Christmas in England is shown in a long red robe with ermine
trim.* Above middle: *A more familiar-looking Santa brings
gifts on a miniature train in this German postcard.*
Above left: *A German card from the early 1900s shows Santa's
gentler appearance starting to emerge from earlier depictions.*

L ong before the days of e-mails and cell
phones, friends around the world took time
to handwrite their greetings on postcards,
especially for the holidays. They had no other choices.

Barbara Kissinger, a good friend of Santa Claus from
southeast Iowa, has been taken in by the charm of the
colorful cards.

What amazes her is that sending postcards was a
worldwide phenomenon. It has touched people in so
many countries—Germany, France, Russia, England,
Slovenia, Czechoslovakia, Sweden, Norway, Denmark,
Finland, Estonia, the Netherlands, Portugal, Spain,
Luxembourg, Liechtenstein, Belgium, Hungary, and
Romania, along with the United States.

"I have always been a kid at heart," she says with
a sparkle in her eye. Now in her early 70s, she
remembers when her love of Santa came to the
forefront of her life because of a simple event. "In
the early 1980s, my mother suggested that I look at
a *Reader's Digest* piece about the history of Santa.

Written by Carol McGarvey ✦ *Photographs by Andy Lyons*

Üdvözlet a Mikulástól!

VESELÉ Vianoce!

I started exploring the whole notion of gift givers, and it took over my life."

Her interests took her down two paths. She started collecting antique Christmas postcards to get ideas for wood figures of various Gift-Givers (the name of her business), which she created, carved, and painted from 1983 to 1996. Each was labeled with name, country, and year. "Wood items were so popular right then, so it was a perfect medium," Barbara explains.

The Santa figures were an instant hit. She produced 1,000 the first year and up to 2,000 per year during her cottage industry's heyday. She made 16 different versions, each holding a bag of goodies or a toy, such as a jack-in-the-box.

From the postcards she interpreted her folk art figures. For example, there is an 1898 Old St. Nick, packing a bag for his Christmas journey. He is

From top left: A card from Hungary shows Santa loading gifts onto a small sled. A card from the Czech Republic is interesting due to the color of the cloak. A postcard from Russia before the revolution is from the era of 1900 to 1910. The gift giver from Finland delivers gifts from a basket in a card from the early 1900s. A card from Hungary shows a bare tree and gifts on a low sled. A highly embellished card was printed in Germany for the American holiday market.

depicted placing a blackboard, a teddy bear, and a toy horse in the bag. He wears a styled red suit. Then there's a 1908 Père Nöel, the French Father Christmas, wearing a green robe with ermine trim and carrying a green velvet bag. There is also a 1970 Grandfather Frost, the gift giver of the Festival of Winter in Russia,

Hauskaa Joulua

Boldog karácsonyi ünnepeket

A HAPPY CHRISTMAS to YOU

SANTA CLAUS SERIES 404

wearing a soft blue robe and carrying a staff and a white velvet bag.

Later she made only the faces of various historical gift givers in ornament form. Barbara sold the figures by mail order and through 100 stores in 30 states. She kept up with the orders with the help of 13 people in her own dining room and basement, along with some in their own mini workshops. For example one woman set up shop in her own home, making bag after bag for the figures to hold gifts.

"My late husband, Gerald, put up with me and with the cottage industry in our home for so many years," she remembers fondly.

Barbara no longer makes the wood figures, but she still collects the postcards that gave her inspiration. She has about 600 cards depicting Santa and Christmas themes, along with others from Valentine's Day and

Wie die Tanne immer grün
Soll Dir Lieb' und Freundschaft blüh'n!

Above: *A German postcard shows Pelznichol walking in the woods with a tree on his back.*

FRÖHLICHE WEIHNACHTEN

Wishing you a MERRY CHRISTMAS

XMAS GREETING

Christmas Greetings.

Easter. They were the perfect collection for her to take along when she moved to a smaller home. She has paid from $10 to $150 for individual cards and now often does her shopping on eBay on the Internet. She is still searching for some elusive ones that she'd love to have.

Barbara is amazed by the color and reproduction of the cards, especially her German favorites. "The papers and the printing process, chromolithography, were rich and vibrant. The Germans, masters at the art, also printed cards for other countries. The largest time for such postcards was from the late 1800s to the 1930s," Barbara explains. "Some of the cards were still made in Europe into the 1960s, '70s, and '80s."

While the height of sending postcards dwindled after the 1930s, she has seen some cards that were still used into the 1980s by formerly Communist countries.

Opposite, clockwise: A German card shows the gift bearer at the door as children watch. Two American cards have a decidedly European look. An English card includes a tree full of toys. Above from left: A card from the Netherlands features Julemand as the gift bearer. This card is American, but has an interesting graphic quality. A Russian greeting card shows Santa bringing gifts by boat.

"I like them all, but the detail of the German-produced ones is special to me," she says.

The Christmas historian likes the links between Santa Claus, the Christ child, and the Belsnickle gift givers. Not all was sweetness and light at the holidays, warns Barbara. German Belsnickles doled out punishments as well as treats. She shows cards featuring Krampus, a devil-like character who carried naughty children in Germany and Austria into the forest. He makes a lump of coal seem like a welcome gift.

A close look at some of Barbara's postcards tells holiday stories from the world over. With the German cards, for example, Santa Claus usually doesn't wear the fur-trimmed red suit of jacket and pants that Americans have come to know. He wears a longish coat or cloak. Or sometimes he wears gilded vestments on these pages of the past, as the cards seem to be. "Cards with figures wearing cloaks other than red usually are more valuable because they are earlier," Barbara says. Other colors might be brown, blue, green, and white.

In chronological order, the cards show the evolution of the gift-giving figures from elfish spirits full of mischief to honored saints to roly-poly commercial beings. The figures weren't always jolly. Some of the earlier German ones wear a stern face. English Santas generally aren't as chubby, but they appear just as friendly.

Barbara explains that many of the early gift givers are depicted on cards walking their rounds, since flying with reindeer came much later. Some ride donkeys or early cars or boats; others pull period sleds.

Postcards from the golden age—around the turn of the 20th century—sometimes feature tinsel or gold trim, die-cut sections, or movable parts.

An American printer, Louis Prang, an immigrant from what is now Poland, is credited with perfecting the postcards to an art form. He printed his first holiday cards in the early 1870s and sold them in England, where sending greeting cards was already commonplace. He started selling them in America in 1875, two years after the introduction of the penny postcard. A standard letter or greeting card cost 3 cents to mail. The cards were an instant hit, and Prang couldn't meet the demand. He became known

Above from left: An English card shows stockings hung at the foot of a bed. This postcard is from Australia but printed in England. St. Nicolas in the Netherlands is a vision in white. A God Jul card in Sweden is unusual in that elves or tomptes are normally shown at the holidays. A German card includes reindeer in the holiday scene. An Irish postcard made in England shows Father Christmas distributing gifts.

as the "Father of the American Christmas card." At his peak Prang was printing more than 5 million cards per year.

The international postcards, not surprisingly, depicted differing holiday traditions in various countries. In wishing a *Joyeux Noel,* French cards showed feather trees with few decorations, and Father Christmas

God Jul.

Fröhliche Weihnachten!

Wishing you a happy Christmas

(also called Père Nöel) was tall and thin like the trees. He was the secular Christmas figure, as opposed to the religious figure, Saint Nicholas.

English cards showed Father Christmas often with a holly wreath on his head and accompanied by the Christmas Fairy. German postcards, with their *Fröhliche Weihnachten* greetings, sometimes showed St. Nicholas or Der Weihnachtsmann (the Christmas Man) traveling with Christkindl, an earthly Christ child, often depicted as an angelic little girl. In other German regions St. Nicholas is accompanied by the Belsnickle (or Pelznickel), a stern-faced character. In Finland, the gift giver wishes *Hauskaa Joulua* and brings presents in a basket, not a bag.

Barbara thinks it is sad that the notion of sending postcards has faded from popularity. But that's why it's important to keep learning by treasuring them.

CHRISTMAS GREETINGS.

Above: *This American card shows an early depiction of Santa's sleigh and reindeer on the roof.*

Santas & Sleds

SLEDS OF ALL SIZES, SHAPES, AND COLORS DECORATE THIS HOLIDAY HOME, PAYING TRIBUTE TO WINTERTIME FUN AND SANTA HIMSELF.

Yes, Santa Claus may have one huge sleigh that he and his reindeer put to work on their marathon toy-delivering trip around the world on Christmas Eve. But he's got nothing on Mary Jo and Bob Frazier.

The folk art-loving Fraziers live with a collection of wonderful sleds and miniature sleighs in every room of their cozy home. They display full-size children's sleds on walls throughout their house, and groups of miniature varieties rest on shelves for impact. Some of the miniature versions are thought to be salesmen's samples or, more likely, doll sleds that replicated an owner's larger one.

"Our love of sleds—for both of us—goes back to our childhood," Mary Jo explains. "Our land was pretty flat, so sledding meant going down big piles of snow that had been plowed after a big snowstorm." Her imaginary mountains provided many hours of outdoor fun.

Bob, however, could slide the hills in a river valley not far away. "We made our own fun. This was before television and video games. Between sledding and ice skating, we spent lots of time outdoors."

For both, even now, autumn and winter are their favorite times of the year because those are enjoyable

times to be outside. They started collecting sleds in 1989 and have been on the quest for more ever since.

SLED SPECIFIC

Sleds are gender-specific according to their style, Mary Jo explains. "A girl's sled is higher because she often sat up to slide down a hill. A boy's sled, however, is lower to the ground because a boy might be expected to belly flop onto his sled to ride down a hill."

The two say that sleds, like many other antiques they enjoy, developed in the Northeast United States. At first sleds were utilitarian, used to pull items from one place to another or to haul firewood. Sometimes boxes were built on the tops of sleds so that items wouldn't fall off when going up or down a hill. The Fraziers own some of those sleds, indicated by holes on top of a sled where the box attached.

Written by Carol McGarvey ✦ *Photographs by Andy Lyons*

Right: A painted sled makes a holiday grouping with several Santa Claus figures. Opposite: This elaborate sled measures only 6 inches in length, and the seat part slides open to reveal a storage space inside. The Fraziers speculate that it held candies or short pencils when it was new. Its playful design is an example of pyrography, or burned wood, which was a Victorian pastime around the turn of the 20th century. Below right: Bob and Mary Jo Frazier celebrate their special ties to the winter months and their remembrances of the fun of sledding.

Later the fun began, and sleds became toys for red-cheeked children to make the most of a winter day. Around 1860, Mary Jo says, toy sleds started to be painted and decorated with scenes. Companies in Maine, New York, and Pennsylvania, among others, jumped on board the fun. The company whose stamp and name appear most often on antique sleds is the Paris Manufacturing Company of Paris, Maine.

Their assortment of small sleds, likely from around the 1920s, may be doll sleds. "Some families would make sure a little girl's doll had a sled to match the child's sled," Mary Jo points out. Those sleds have survived, of course, because those sleds weren't usually subjected to hard wear and weather. The Paris Manufacturing Company continued operating until the late 1980s.

A closer look at the children's sleds shows that some had carved wood handholds for good gripping. Still others had cutout places for hands to hang on tightly.

The couple enjoys traveling to antiques shows in New England, where it's still possible to find a sled or two. By now they know other individuals with sled interests as well. Mary Jo smiles about a trip a few years ago. "We were waiting in an airport, and I was holding a sled we had purchased. A little lady, likely about 80 years old, gingerly asked if she could take a look at the front of the sled. 'Ah, that looks so much like the wonderful sled I had as a little girl,' she said. Many of us have good memories of sledding."

A Christmas Classic

While they might look like whimsically designed, almost childlike ornaments of today, these chenille and pipe cleaner Santa tree ornaments, *above*, are actually reproductions of some ornaments produced more than 50 years ago. Made from very inexpensive materials, these tiny Santa ornaments were purchased for pennies at general stores or dime stores. They were usually purchased in multiples and hung on the tree or tied to packages.

Santa boots in various sizes, *below*, are fashioned of papier-mâché and pressed cardboard. These fun-to-display pieces were very inexpensive to buy and were available from the 1930s until the late 1950s. Mary Jo often puts candy canes, cinnamon sticks, or candies in them during the holiday season.

Even though the sign says "No Sliding," Mary Jo and Bob Frazier display a portion of their antique sled collection. These hang on a wall over a stairway to the home's lower level.

Below right: A faded ceramic Santa Claus holding cinnamon sticks is special because it belonged to Bob's father.

While a stamp on the back identifies many of the vintage sleds with "Paris Manufacturing Company," others might bear a name, such as "Iris" or "No. 61." Some sleds were known by their color or detail, with names such as Black Beauty or White Star. The Fraziers' research has shown that rotating worktables were used in assembly lines at sled-making operations. When one function was completed, the table was turned so that the sled could go to the next phase of production.

A REAL FIND

One special sled that hangs in a guest bedroom, referred to as "Bob's find," is a delicately curved little girl's sled found in Waynesville, Ohio. With curlicues and bells in the runners, it is painted a creamy white. From their research the Fraziers know it likely is a Snow Fairy sled from the late 1800s. For some reason Bob felt the urge to use a pocketknife and start carefully scraping off the paint. Underneath he found a colorful floral scene stenciled on the sled. Further research confirmed the name and the source, with an estimated date of 1870–1880. Other common painted motifs included ocean scenes, roses, and fern fronds.

DECKING THE HALLS

Mary Jo and Bob have given their newer home a country farmhouse feel by using warm, vibrant colors throughout. Deep red walls in the living and dining rooms show off sleds and graphic game boards. Inviting wingback chairs and love seats are upholstered in red and rich yellow toile fabric. Gingham valances in the same hues enhance large bay windows with a bit of color.

In the kitchen and adjoining

hearth room, navy
walls show off more sleds and also a collection
of spice boxes. The master bedroom, in taupe and
navy, provides another backdrop for showcasing the
couple's variety of sleds.

The couple also owns a variety of baby and doll
sleighs, along with several handsome horse-and-wagon
sets and a number of rocking horses in several sizes.

At the holidays, of course, the toys take center stage
because they often were gifts from Santa Claus. Mary Jo
prefers natural decorations as a backdrop for the toys,
such as Fraser fir trees, evergreen swags, and pinecones.

Like other details of modern life, artistic sleds went
to the wayside when speed became important for
sleds. Also a change to mass production and plastic
materials replaced handmade wood construction and
hand-painted artistic embellishment.

Mary Jo and Bob, however, hold fast to the past and
how it impacted their childhood. "It is important that
we preserve the past," she emphasizes. "We are the
stewards of what went on before us."

*Miniature sleds—likely salesman's samples or doll sleds—act
as a backdrop to papier-mâché Santas from about the 1930s.
Above: A special Santa toy that moves across a table was a gift to
Mary Jo from her grandfather when she was 4 years old. While
some visitors think it's unusual that a sheep is pulling Santa,
Mary Jo says a closer look shows that it's a reindeer that has lost
its antlers.*

These Santa figures are among Leo and Marilyn Smith's favorite pieces. Their exquisite work inspires everyone to feel the spirit of Santa year-round.

Creating Saint Nicholas,

no matter what the medium, is a

heartwarming passion for many.

These devoted artists use their talents

to sculpt, carve, paint, and

craft keepsake-quality characters.

MASTER CRAFTERS

Sculpting a Father Christmas

A LOVE OF SANTA INSPIRES THIS ARTIST TO MOLD MAGIC FROM POLYMER CLAY.

Laura Benge lives on an acreage near a rural community of slightly more than 400 people in north central Iowa. But single-handedly she increases the population of the area by thousands with her Santa Claus figures, until the figures leave to spread holiday cheer to homes far and wide. No problem. She just makes more. For 20 years she has sculpted various figures from polymer clay to bring a smile to people's lives.

"I started out making miniatures," she explains. "Most were 2-inch occupational designs honoring various professions, such as teaching, nursing, or fire fighting. I sold them at craft shows and some shops." Somewhere along the line—she doesn't remember when—the figures got bigger and turned into Santa characters with exquisite detail.

Most of Laura's figures range from 6 to 8 inches, and each one takes on its own personality. "I tend to make old world-looking Santas with a whimsical touch. I love adding the details to give them individuality," Laura says.

Written by Carol McGarvey ✦ *Photographs by Andy Lyons*

Hats, garments, and beards vary. These two carry American flags, which Laura also sculpted. Opposite: Two of Laura's figures show the depth of her detail. One holds two dolls. The other carries a birdhouse.

Her love of the season inspires her art. Laura has no idea how long it takes to make one figure because she never makes a whole one from start to finish. She creates a dozen heads at a time. Those with larger noses remind her of her grandfather. The roly-poly shapes bring to mind her late father.

EVERY DETAIL

A word of advice: Avoid dropping in on Laura when she's making eyeballs or you might become a bit unnerved. She forms clay eyeballs, paints them white, and bakes them before inserting them into the heads. It's a little eerie to see a group of the heads without eyes.

Laura doesn't use sophisticated tools to sculpt her holiday magic—a crafts knife, a paring knife, a nut pick, and the end of a paintbrush help her create. She makes a mold and the pieces are molded of resin.

She paints the clothing and details of each Santa. For beards she uses real or clay fur. She's constantly on the lookout for items for the Santas to sit on or to hold, including wagons, rockers, sleds, bells, Christmas trees, dolls, or basketballs. Often she sculpts American flags for them to wave. Besides Santas, she also makes roly-poly figures and snowmen.

Laura's Santas are sold in shops in Larchmont,

"I even talk to them. Can you believe it?" Laura confesses. It's OK. Her husband Rusty encourages her work, and the children, Justin, Nolan, and Molly, have grown up with the characters in their home.

Laura says her enjoyment of this artwork is probably genetic. "My mom, Eunice Corcoran, has always enjoyed painting with watercolors and oils, so all of us kids seem to have inherited some artistic interests." Laura studied commercial art and business but professionally worked on the numbers side. Now she combines her artistic skills and business sense in Whimsical Creations.

ALWAYS LOVES CHRISTMAS

Christmas has always been a special time of year for Laura. As the youngest of nine children—with a 19-year span from first to last—the holidays were full of anticipation. "With that much space between us all, some of the older siblings were out of the house while I was growing up. I looked forward to Christmas when everyone came home to the farm. Gift giving was a big part of our family." She says she was also influenced by *The Night Before Christmas*. "I remember being so excited at the holidays."

Opposite: Laura Benge's sculpted figures take on all kinds of looks, from traditional to fanciful. Some hold elves, while others tote baskets of kittens. Right: *This Santa tries out a chimney for size.* Above left: *Surrounded by tools, Laura brings her Santas to life.*

California, Branson, Missouri, and Raleigh, North Carolina. She also does one craft show each year, War Eagle in Arkansas. Her figures sell for $75 to $150 each. Because there are collectors among Laura's followers, she started making limited series of her roly-poly figures. Characters are retired every three years.

For her state's high school athletic commission, she has designed Santas holding sports balls with the group's logo. The commission sends the figures to other states' groups as a holiday favor.

Laura spends 30 to 70 hours each week creating her characters. "Sure, there are days I tire of them, but then I get all excited making others. I love Christmas."

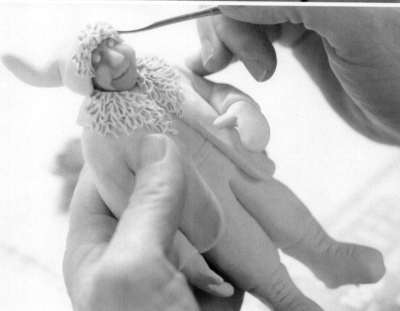

Opposite: *A jolly Santa figure carries teddy bears, every child's favorite huggable item.* Left: *The Santa holds a doll's hand while sitting on top of a snowball.* Above top: *Making heads and eyeballs is how Laura starts the process of building personalities for her Santas.* Above: *Laura sculpts detail on a Santa before painting.*

Salt Lake Santas

CREATED IN A TINY TOWN IN UTAH AND DRESSED IN MAGICAL CLOTHES, THESE SANTAS ARE FASHIONED FROM WOOD AND WONDER.

With shelves chock-full of satin, silk, burlap, velvet, and brocade, Susan Ewing's studio seems like it must be in the North Pole. Instead the Utah native weaves her Christmas magic in Highland, a town about 40 miles south of Salt Lake City.

For 15 years the artist has fashioned Santa figures, angels, fairies, and witches. "I had been a tole painter for some time, but I felt the need to do something dimensional in my work," she explains. "Once, at a store, I saw a set of rotary carving tools. I thought that sounded fun to explore. My husband, Steve, and I started to work with the tools and learned how to carve. It was lots of fun, and I became hooked."

She makes only a few of the other fanciful characters and concentrates on Santa Claus figures. "Since I was a little girl, I have always loved Christmas. It's a magical and wonderful time, no matter how old you are."

Susan devotes major amounts of time to her work, fashioning 12 to 15 detailed Santas each year. "While my ability has greatly improved, my speed has not," she admits. Each 2-foot tall figure is signed, numbered, and titled.

The artist doesn't work in an assembly-line fashion, preferring to produce each character from start to

Above: *Whee!* Santa Inadvertently Discovers the Luge *honors the 2002 Winter Olympics in Salt Lake City.* Opposite: *This is Susan's favorite Santa face on her beloved Bellsnickle.*

Produced by Nicole Lozier ✦ *Written by Carol McGarvey* ✦ *Photographs by Stuart Ruckman*

finish. "The whole process seems to flow better that way for the way I work," she explains. "By the time I'm done, I have spent so much time with each one that he feels like a friend." Some of the characters come together flawlessly, and some require more time and patience.

Susan ruminates a bit on each one before starting. "I really don't have an overall plan for each figure. I just start in. I'm always looking at people and at pictures and photographs for interesting facial features that I can work into the Santas. The face is so important. I let that guide me."

She starts the head with a piece of basswood and carves away what she doesn't need. Sometimes she fashions hands from wood as well. "Somehow I can 'see' the head as I carve," she says. "I just can feel it as I go along."

Her husband is very supportive. Steve keeps the tools in working order and even built Susan a separate building behind their home for her carving. "It's just one room, about 15 by 15 feet, but it's the perfect spot for carving. I might not go out there for a day or two, but when I do and I smell the wood, I feel right at home." Sometimes Susan works eight hours a day on her Santas and other times only four hours a week.

FASHION FORWARD

As the process goes forward, Susan is likely to be in her workroom, a bedroom-turned-studio. In the room is shelf after shelf and stack after stack of silks, brocades, velvets, and wool fabrics awaiting their turn to bring the Santa figures to life. "I'm truly addicted," Susan admits with a chuckle. "I scour yard sales, thrift stores, estate sales, and order from catalogs. I'm always on the lookout for recycled fur, vintage fabrics, and sometimes new fabrics for the clothing." When she can find it, the artist looks for vintage handwork to embellish her characters. When she can't find it, she creates her own. She also is on the lookout for toys or any other details that might be incorporated into her figures. Wool for the beards of each Santa is imported from England.

One of her main tools is her hot-glue gun—"And I've got the burn marks to prove it."

Susan feels a calling to her work. "I have always loved art, and that is in my genes, I believe. I have found out that my great-grandmothers were prolific in needlework and that my great-grandfathers had a way with wood."

She is inspired by events around her as well. One of her figures, called *Santa Inadvertently Discovers the Luge*, is an ode to the 2002 Winter Olympics, which took

Below: *Susan fashions a head as she starts a new character.* Below bottom: *A wallboard shows part of the artist's array of fabrics, ready for the picking.* Opposite: *Susan made* Grandfather Frost *for her son when he was on a mission trip in Russia.*

Above: *Mr. and Mrs. Claus kick up their heels in* The Christmas Celebration. Opposite: *The artist's newest Santa is* Pére Noël.

place in Salt Lake City. Another one, called *Grandfather Frost*, honors her son's Mormon mission time spent in the Ukraine.

Sometimes real people work their way through her ideas and her busy fingers. One time when she finished a face, she realized she had duplicated the face of a relative. Steve agreed. "Why, that's Aunt Dorothy," he said when he saw the face. Ever mindful of the true meaning of Christmas, Susan strives to ensure that her figures aren't construed as too commercial. One figure, named *The Symbols of Christmas,* employs simple and direct symbols, such as an unadorned tree and a

Below: *Susan Ewing fashions a head as she starts a new character.* Below bottom: *The artist's hands are busy at work in her wood studio.* Right above: *In* The Symbols of Christmas, *the character represents love, the spirit of the holiday.* Opposite: *In* The Christmas Story, *Father Christmas reads the familiar story to a fairy.*

star to glorify the Savior. "Also," she says, "Santa is about love, and that's what Christmas honors."

While Susan has done custom orders, she prefers not to work that way. "I don't want anyone disappointed if I didn't interpret an idea they had in mind."

After working with her figures for a month or more, she finds that it's OK to let them go to other homes. By then, she's starting on the next ones. The only Santa she has kept is the first one she ever made. "Thank goodness, I have improved immensely."

For 20 years she had a partnership with several others in a shop called Through the Grapevine. The shop was sold, so now she markets her figures through other stores, a mailing list, and her Web site.

Her one-of-a-kind figures start at $1,000. "It is such an honor for me that collectors appreciate the work that I enjoy so much," says the modest designer.

Mr. & Mrs. Smith Carve Santas

WOOD, PAINT, AND IMMEASURABLE TALENT ARE ALL IT TAKES TO MAKE THESE ONE-OF-A-KIND SANTAS.

In Santa circles, it seems that the work of Leo and Marilyn Smith is just about as well-known as the "right jolly old elf" himself. For 34 years the Wisconsin couple has carved and painted its way into the hearts of Christmas lovers all over the world.

That's not surprising, says Marilyn, the painting partner of the duo. "Like other families, Christmas has always been very special to us, especially Leo's side. All family members exchange personalized handmade gifts. It's a lovely tradition."

"I'm pretty much self-taught," Leo says with pride. His distinctive carving style has people telling him that many of the Santas he fashions somehow end up looking like him—tall and lean with angular features.

"I don't mean for that to happen, but it just does," he says. He is humbled by the devotion that collectors have for the work that he and Marilyn complete. "We're modest and we're Midwesterners, so it's hard to accept compliments."

Marilyn notes that her husband puts an unusual realistic quality into his carvings, especially the faces that are brought to life even more with painting. "Many times our folk art figures resemble a person that we have known or even someone we haven't yet met. This happened with the piece called *Toymaker Santa* that Leo made in 1990. A couple years later Leo was doing an in-store appearance, and the owner of the shop looked so much like the *Toymaker Santa*. It looked as if the owner had posed as Leo's model.

It has been said that our work seems to have an inner life, that the pieces could almost come to life if one let one's imagination take over." The Smiths keep their workshops buzzing in Fountain City, Wisconsin, about 40 miles north of LaCrosse. The term is

Opposite: Winter Claus, *with his European look, is one of carver Leo's treasured items.* Left: White Deer Santa *honors the albino deer of Wisconsin.*

Written by Carol McGarvey ✦ *Photographs by Andy Lyons*

workshops—plural—because Leo carves and Marilyn paints in separate studios about two blocks apart. They insist it works better that way. "We work in separate buildings together," they conclude with a smile. Leo's studio is adjacent to the couple's home. Marilyn's is adjacent to their retail shop down the street. Both studios look down on the Mississippi River and across to the bluffs of their native Minnesota. Leo draws inspiration from looking at the river views as he carves from Wisconsin white pine.

The couple introduces up to 15 new pieces each year. Not all designs make the cut of course. Some must be worked on and revised, and both artists have veto power.

Before the process comes to that point, however, they do plenty of research into art history and ancient times to discover the magnificent details appropriate to the various pieces. "A picture may trigger an idea," says Leo, explaining how limited editions originate. "Also we must look at the notion of just how many collectors might want a certain piece." To keep the inventory fresh, various pieces are retired each year.

Besides Santa figures, the couple creates Pilgrims, angels, nature pieces, and more. The process is a firm concept with a beginning, an end, and a perspective.

Sometimes Leo does a pencil sketch to lock in his idea, and periodically he makes a model in clay to bring a concept to life. Generally figures are 10 to 15 inches tall. Each one takes a different amount of time, depending on the complexity of the details.

Leo might have a relatively easy experience with carving a piece, and Marilyn might have difficulties

Above right: Santa Fisherman on Creel. Right: *Marilyn and Leo Smith stand with one of their larger characters, the* Lion and Lamb Santa. Opposite, clockwise: Santa on Yule Reindeer. Northwoods Santa *in his Paul Bunyan-style shirt*. Milk Run Santa *honors the Dairy State*. Northwoods Santa *in Canoe*.

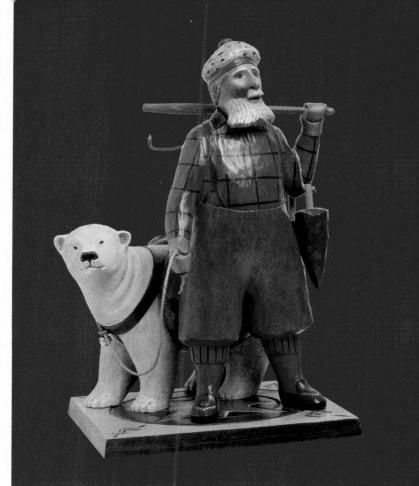

Left: *In the foreground are* Fisherman Santa *and* Santa Skier.

Above: Santa of Peace *holds the world in his hands.*

GLAD TIDINGS

Toy MAKER

getting just the right coloration. And then the reverse might happen. Projects vary so much that an average time to complete a piece can't be calculated.

Marilyn uses water-base acrylic paints to complete a carving. Only after a piece passes their stringent jury of two is it ready to be made into a resin mold.

The two have made "hundreds and hundreds" of pieces since 1971, and they have a collection of their own work for reference. For a time their work was part of the Department 56 and Midwest of Cannon Falls collections, but now they're on their own. "People find us pretty easily," Leo says. "Somehow they get to this little long narrow town of 980 on the river road. Cars go through, and then they turn around and come back to our little brick building. You notice those things in small towns."

The Smiths are proud of the personal service they offer to their retail shop customers. "We seem to be known for that, and people appreciate that part of our

business," Leo points out. "It's kind of an old-fashioned way of doing business. Many times we get letters from people who have visited our shop, telling us it was the highlight of their trip."

While many customers shop in the store during a time of special celebration, others seek out a Smith piece in time of crisis. For example, one man was going to have brain surgery at the Mayo Clinic in Rochester, Minnesota, and sent his son to the Smiths' shop to purchase an angel for his wife. "Wow," says Leo. "You wouldn't think if you were having brain surgery that you would be thinking about buying one of our pieces, but he did."

Their pieces cost up to $300 retail, and as much as $1,000 per piece on the secondary market, Marilyn says. The two say they have a sensory barometer of what pieces will be hits with collectors. "Usually the pieces that we like the best, so do collectors," Leo says. Sometimes they'll "float" a piece in their

From opposite left: Glad
Tidings Santa. Dancing
Santa. Toymaker Santa.
Stars and Stripes Santa.
Santa and Mrs. Claus.
Gardening Santa.
Left: Great Plains Santa.

unscientific test market just to get a reaction. They find that customers are more than willing to share opinions. "When the customers get excited, we do too," says the longtime carver.

Do they ever get tired of creating Santa figures? "We could never let down our collectors," Leo explains. "It is such a satisfying feeling to know that we have collectors and friends all over the world."

When Christmas comes, they're exhausted but energized by carrying on the tradition of gathering their family for the holidays. "We have four children, and they're all artistic in their own ways. It's fun to know that is genetic," says their proud mother.

The Smiths' favorite pieces, without a doubt, are the latest pieces, the ones they have just completed.

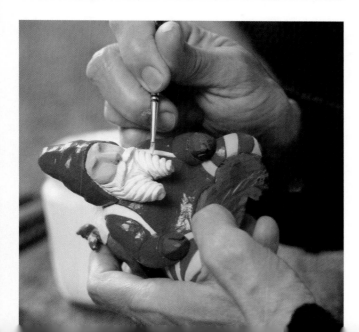

Opposite: North Pole Santa *rides a polar bear and carries fish in his backpack.* Above left: *Leo carves away on a new project.* Middle left: *Wood chips and knives are the tools of Leo's art.* Left: *Marilyn uses acrylic paints to bring life to one of Leo's carvings.* Above: *This playful figure of Santa enticing a pig with an ear of corn is called* Boar and Peace.

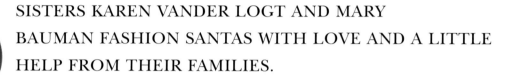

Family Ties

SISTERS KAREN VANDER LOGT AND MARY
BAUMAN FASHION SANTAS WITH LOVE AND A LITTLE
HELP FROM THEIR FAMILIES.

Everyone has an opinion, and the families of
Wisconsin Santa crafters Karen Vander Logt
and Mary Bauman are more than happy to
share their thoughts (and offer some input) on the
sisters' creations.

"My entire family gets into the act," says Karen. Sons
Ben, Jace, and Aaron help their mom with everything
from how a Santa should look to which toys should be
in a particular Santa's bag. Aaron also insisted his
mother and aunt start a Web site to showcase their
Santas. Mary's daughter, Drena, designed their business

Right: *Sisters Karen Vander Logt and Mary Bauman express
their passion for the holidays and love of art in their handcrafted
Santa Clauses.* Above right: *Looking as if he's striding through a
London alley, Mary's* My English Gentleman *wears a long brown
and white wool herringbone coat with matching cap.* Above:
*Pennsylvania artisan Rich Castrina handcrafted this shiny red
cutter sleigh for Karen. Her son Ben made the small toy jester
peering out of Santa's sack.*

Written by Chris Ellibee ✦ Photographs by John Reed Forsman

A quartet of the sisters' Father Christmases (Karen's two on the left, Mary's two on the right) in glittering white and gold robes stands at attention in front of the Vander Logt's living room fireplace.

logo and brochures. Even their husbands pitch in with the work. Rick Vander Logt and Joe Bauman drive their spouses to Santa shows, assist with setting up displays, and act as sympathetic shoulders to lean on when Santa-making swings into full production each fall. "Sometimes I even get Joe to model for me," Mary says lightheartedly.

In 1999 Karen and Mary were looking for a home-based activity they both could do, something incorporating their artistic nature and love of Christmas.

They settled on making Santa Clauses when Mary was at Karen's house and the duo happened to be reading copies of *Better Homes and Gardens Santa Claus* magazine. "We both looked at each other and said, 'We can do this.'" Karen says, "It combines everything we like to do—art, shopping, and sewing—into one thing." Their business, Visions of an Olde Friend, was born.

DIFFERENT LOOKS

Karen and Mary each make Santas, and their unique creations have similarities and subtle differences. The sisters look for inspiration from vintage Santa postcards and pictures. Or they might get an idea for a Santa Claus from someone they see on television or pass by while shopping at the mall.

The first step is crafting the heads and bodies. Karen and Mary use like processes. They begin heads with a ball of tinfoil covered in polymer clay. Then they sculpt the faces before firing them in the oven.

It is in the faces where one notices the differences in the sisters' art. Mary's Santas have a dreamy expression,

Opposite: *In this loving vignette, Karen choreographed a holiday dance between Santa and Mrs. Claus.* Above right: *Karen's Santa Claus Stitch in Time holds a stocking ready to fill with holiday goodies.* Right: *Karen curls the hair of her figure's beard with small rollers. Curls give extra dimension and character to her Santas' faces. One of the St. Nicholas figures in the background wears a purple cape made from a coat that belonged to her husband's grandmother.*

while Karen's faces have an old-world look. Each has its own personality. "Many of our customers say that the Santas look so real, they look like they should breathe," Mary says. Bodies take shape with dowels and wire wrapped in fluffy cotton batting. Then, as both sisters agree, the real work begins. "Designing and sewing the clothes takes the most time in the process," says Karen. Each Santa gets an original outfit cut and sewn from new or vintage fabrics, furs, and accessories found by searching fabric stores, vintage clothing stores, and antiques shops.

It generally takes the sisters two to three weeks to make one of their collectible Santas. Heights range from 14 to 38 inches. Sales are made at shows and on their Web site.

"We try to attend two shows each year. One we try not to miss is the Holiday Market in Kohler, Wisconsin, held in early November. It's close to home," Mary says, "but most of our sales are made through our Web site."

Karen and Mary have a remarkable sense of community and feel strongly about giving back and sharing their good fortune. For the past several years, they each have donated one Santa for a silent auction benefiting the Interfaith Caregiving Network in Waukesha, Wisconsin, a service that assists senior citizens and disabled adults.

The sisters agree that the best part of their work is the joy of watching customers look at their Santas for the first time and the positive responses they receive. "They're our babies," Karen says.

Above left: *Regal in a black Persian lamb hat and a jacket with gold epaulets, one of Mary's Santas holds a small drum-playing teddy bear.* Left: *Mary uses a glue gun to apply silken mohair to a Santa. Mary signs and numbers each figure before attaching the mohair.* Opposite: *A jolly Santa finishes a cheery snowman by giving him a small branch arm in* Mary's Polar Pals.

A group of Teri Embrey's
"Santas for the Soul" show
her attention to detail on
the quilts they carry.
Opposite: *Even the cover on
this carved book, called
"Midnight Magic," offers
a tranquil scene.*

Santas for the Soul

THIS MERRY WANDERER SPREADS HOLIDAY CHEER
WITH LOVINGLY CARVED CHARACTERS.

Santa's magical powers are never in question. Few, however, talk of his healing powers. Teri Embrey, an artist and wood-carver from Seattle, is an exception. She knows.

"Santa brought me back from the serious depression," she says. After a series of devastating happenings in her life, she gave up her love of art for a time.

"I always had drawn and painted, and Santa always had been a forceful spirit in my work. My grandmother was indeed a 'Christmas freak,' and it rubbed off on me. She made our family Christmases in West Virginia so special," Teri explains. "Everybody wanted her for a grandmother."

Teri particularly remembers a plastic Santa that her grandmother put on the front porch every year. "It was a symbol to me of all that she was." Because of that tie, Teri collected Santas and painted Santa figures on canvas.

Her father, a woodworker, provided an impetus for Teri's carving. She used some of his leftover wood pieces and also found branches to carve. After meeting a carver at a folk art gallery in Chicago, Teri was hooked on the skill. "It spoke to me."

Then a series of events in her family and personal life put her into a deep depression, and her artwork

Written by Carol McGarvey ✦ *Photographs by Mike Jensen*

Opposite: *The lace-style details created with a wood-burning tool form a delicate border around Santa's sleeves and the edge of his garment.* Above top: *Teri applies finishing embellishments to a Santa in her Seattle studio.* Above: *Teri's Santas appear to peek out of treasured books. She likes to combine comforting items, such as Santa, quilts, and books.*

went by the wayside. A few years later, however, carving Santas became therapy to heal her. Her interesting figures, which she calls Santas for the Soul, came from the depths of her struggles. As she carves them, they emerge from within her spirit.

"Each one of my guys evolves as I go along. I don't start with a plan. I absolutely love what I do, and it's just incredible that others do too." As Teri grows emotionally, so do her figures.

"People tend to see the soul in my pieces," she says. "They tell me that they evoke memories of their own childhood and their own life. What wonderful feedback!"

Sometimes it is hard for Teri to let go of the figures. "But my joy is that they are going to someone who will love them. They are going to a safe place."

Coincidentally, that's how it is with Teri too. This year she moved from Ohio to Seattle, Washington to start a new life. "I came here several times a year to visit friends and decided it would be a good place for me to start over."

Teri's pieces generally end up being 9 to 12 inches tall. They retail for $150 to $400 and are available in a number of galleries and shops around the country. She carves them from basswood, Northern pine, or cottonwood bark. She often carves five or six pieces and then switches into another artistic mode to paint them. She works with acrylic paints and water-base stains. For some accents, such as vines or lace-looking trim, she embellishes the carvings with woodburned details.

While some artists prefer to be able to walk away from their studio at the end of the day, Teri lives in hers. "I like to always be able to be ready when an idea hits me. If that's at 4 a.m., so be it. I'm right there with my tools at hand."

You won't find Christmas toys or tinsel on Teri's figures. Each figure offers a quiet personality, full of solace and inner joy. "My guys offer gifts to comfort the soul—a comforting quilt to warm it, a favorite old book to nourish it, or just a knowing look from a compassionate friend to bring it strength."

Teri Embrey's Santa's line up in quiet beauty.

She points out that her work brings peace, not holiday glitz. For that reason she hopes the figures will be used to bring joy all year in someone's home, not just at the holidays. "These aren't just eye candy. Hopefully they appear like old friends that feed your soul."

The artist says her Santa figures are about something bigger than the usual notion of Santa Claus. For her they are about the spirit of hope for things that every individual needs in life—kindness, compassion, and giving.

Many of her pieces show ageless Santas wearing long cloaks and holding quilts, another of her passions. "I love antique quilts, especially patch quilts and crazy quilts. Quilts provide such warmth and comfort, so for me, it's natural that they should work with the Santa figures."

Besides the stand-alone figures, she also carves Santas who appear to walk out from the pages of old books. Sometimes she carves and paints quilt designs to decorate the pages and soothing, tranquil scenes for the covers. Often words on the pages further the comforting nature of the pieces, such as "Friends stitch our lives with love."

Teri also collects Santas made by other artists, and her sister babysits some of Teri's pieces. Her daughter and son, also artistic, cherish her work. "It is so cool when your kids appreciate the things that move your soul." Teri's mother has learned to quilt, so they share an artistic bond as well.

The legacy continues. Teri's grandson, Keenan, is sure that Grandma created Santa Claus.

He may be on to something.

Above left: *A gentle and quiet Santa figure draped in fabric provides an uplifting presence. Teri embeds the detail of vines around his cloak with a wood-burning tool.* Left: *The shape of these figures is determined by the found wood that Teri enjoys using, such as cottonwood bark pieces. "Bark is just magic," she says.*

Teri's love of antique fabrics is expressed in her carving of Santas with softly colored patchwork quilts.

The Paintings of Santa

WITH BRUSH IN HAND, THIS TALENTED ARTIST USES
FAMILY AND FRIENDS TO MAKE HER SANTAS COME ALIVE.

Just like beloved artist Norman Rockwell, who captivated readers with his *Saturday Evening Post* magazine cover drawings, illustrator Sue Cornelison uses real people as models for her work, including Santa Claus greeting cards.

"I'm always asking my family members or neighbors to pose for an illustration I'm working on," she says. That way she gets realistic results for portraits or for her day job of illustrating children's books for an educational publisher.

Here's an example: Sue asks a young neighbor boy, just home from a baseball game, to squat down on his haunches for an illustration of a child playing in a mud puddle. Using a digital camera, Sue snaps a shot looking down on his head to get the body proportions correct. For his efforts Sue gives him some ice cream money.

Sue lives in a Victorian home in a small Iowa community about 30 miles south of the state's capital city. "A small town like this lets us listen to the birds sing and the animals wandering around. It's a wide-open space and very inspiring," says Sue.

When she and her husband, Ross, married, he had two daughters. The couple had four more children

Opposite: *Sue's neighbor, Jack Daniels, often is her model for Santa Claus.* Above: *One of Sue's favorite watercolors.*

Written by Carol McGarvey ✦ *Photographs by Andy Lyons*

together, so as they grew there were plenty of models close at hand. Now the children are older and Sue relies on other friends, neighbors, and youngsters in the gymnastics and competitive tumbling team she coaches.

Her Santa model is a local resident. She also draws on the details of her father's face, which she says "has a natural Santa twinkle."

Neighbors often see her outside posing people for her work. "I guess I'm a realist. I need the model to see how the light plays on faces and on muscles and how dresses fold and fall as a person moves."

Oh yes, there was the time that neighbors and passersby saw Ross, her bass-playing jazz musician husband, wearing a dress and posing with a broom handle in the garden. "I was trying to duplicate the look of an old woman hoeing in the garden, and I was desperate," Sue explains. "I was more embarrassed than he was when the kids arrived home with their friends and he was still wearing the dress while he took a phone call. Like the ham that he is, he played it up. I still cringe," she says with a giggle.

A LIFELONG LOVE OF ART

Her artistic roots go back to her childhood in a Chicago suburb. "I always liked drawing, and I became quite adept at working on a retro toy that is enjoying new popularity, Etch-a-Sketch. I especially loved drawing horses," she says. "I truly just never thought that I could make a career from my art."

So instead she started as a science major in wildlife biology, hoping to become a veterinarian. However, the "whole art thing," as she calls it, kept gnawing at her. She followed her heart and spent time at the University of Arizona in Tucson studying painting and drawing.

She even took off alone for Florence, Italy, to study at the School of Studio Art before returning to the midwest to graduate in art education and painting and drawing.

After teaching art and doing freelance illustration work for various publications—and, of course, primarily being

Opposite, top left and right: *Children and animals play a big part in Sue's art.* Opposite, bottom left and right: *Sue loves to add Santa's bag of toys and a tree to her paintings.* Above: *Embellished borders are typical of Sue's work.*

a mother in the 1980s—she became an educational illustrator for children's books. "I love the whimsical drawings I can do," she says. She prefers having text as guidelines for her illustrations.

THE JOY OF GREETING CARDS

Her Christmas card work expanded her craft and new use of different media. "I found that many of my cards focused on angels and different looks for Santa. I really

enjoy Victorian realism, which worked beautifully for the line of holiday cards."

She enjoys working in watercolor, but for print reproduction purposes, she finds that a combination of colored pencils and mineral spirits creates a satisfying medium. "The spirits make the pencil work richer, and they act more like oil paint," she explains. She likes to work in oils too, but the odors and the required drying time slow her down. Acrylic paint that dries quickly has become a better choice when she wants to paint.

At home Sue works in her studio in the living room of her family's large home, built in 1909 for the local banker. "There's a grand piano, fireplace, couch, spinning wheel, and a great bay window for light. I have a huge oak table that I use for a studio table, along with a big easel. There's no problem with the family being in that room," she says with a chuckle. "With no TV or DVD player, that room has little appeal."

The busy artist draws and paints all day, at work and at home. "I just carry big tubs of work back and forth. I like change and taking on new challenges because I can't stand boredom."

Along with her Santa illustrations, Sue favors the Christmas cards she draws featuring lambs, little girls, and one called *Peace on Earth,* complete with doves. She enjoys those with a definite winter theme because, she points out, "Snow makes any illustration look so much better!" She may reproduce some of the cards into posters.

In her Christmas card illustrations, Sue enjoys drawing Santa Claus variations. "Santa is so versatile, and there are endless ways to bring him to life. He's just a wonderful subject!"

Opposite: *Sue adds dots of "snow" using acrylic paint.* Right above: *Striped and checkered borders set off Sue's work with a graphic look.* Right: *The large living room in the Cornelisons' Victorian home makes the perfect studio for the artist.*

Santa & His Helpers

A DREAM OF WORKING TOGETHER TO MAKE EXQUISITE SANTAS HAS COME TRUE FOR TWO TALENTED WOMEN FROM IDAHO.

Just like Santa's waistline, the design business of Kale Bassler and Terrie Wharton keeps expanding. The two live with their families in Post Falls, Idaho, and work about 10 miles away in a studio in Coeur d'Alene, Idaho. The resort area in northern Idaho, about 30 miles east of Spokane, Washington, is known for its winter skiing and summer lake activities.

Their evolution as business partners had an interesting beginning, Kale explains. "We both worked for a supermarket chain in Coeur d'Alene back in about 1980. We started talking, became friends, and realized that we had similar interests, including pottery, stained glass, and fabric crafts." The two went to art shows and discovered they had similar talents and styles.

"We decided that we wanted to try our hand at making things together and marketing our items at shows," Terrie says. "We made sock monkeys, folk art dolls, wooden doll furniture, and floral arrangements."

Opposite: *A grouping of figures shows vintage characters in white, traditional Santas, and elves.* Right: *A closeup of a vintage Santa shows an aging, kindly face.*

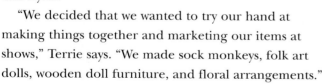

Written by Carol McGarvey ✦ *Photographs by Mike Jensen*

They still kept their day jobs, but their part-time partnership kept growing for nearly 10 years.

About six years ago the supermarket closed. Both Kale and Terrie faced moving to another store in another location. With a giant leap of faith, the two decided the time was right to pursue their artistic ventures on a full-time basis. With their husbands' support, both agreed they had to try their "now or never" operation.

After knowing the market from so many years of doing shows, the two decided to focus on Christmas items. At first they used porcelain faces. Terrie worked on building body armatures from wood and wire, and Kale worked on the clothing styles. Then came the switch to sculpting polymer faces, hands, and feet. They use glass eyes. "I tend to make traditional faces, and Terrie's are a little more stylized," Kale says. Through trial and error, they learned to complement each other's skills and styles.

WORKING TOGETHER

While some artists might think working with someone else would be difficult, Kale and Terrie beg to differ. They give each other's work fresh eyes. Still they retain individuality. For example, Kale sculpts all the elves' distinctive faces, and Terrie creates the faces of the Mountain Men, rugged figures that seem a natural for their Northwest mountain location. Kale tends to do more traditional looks, and Terrie's pieces have a "quirkier" appearance, they both point out.

They make 200 to 300 figures each year, with retail prices from \$125 to \$1,000. They take their characters to large retail shows and wholesale gift markets, where they have developed a large following.

Besides traditional Santa Claus pieces, they also create a line of vintage pieces dressed in white, Mountain Men, and a group of playful elves. They do custom pieces, sometimes incorporating fur coats or clothing pieces that clients want placed on the figure. They also have designed Santa riding on a rocket ship, wearing a Hawaiian shirt, and playing a grand piano.

For beards they use Tibetan lamb's wool, sheepskin wool, mohair, or Icelandic wool. For customers who prefer something other than wool, they also offer a synthetic choice.

Expansion created the need for more space. Initially, they worked in a room at Kale's house. Then

Opposite: *These figures, about 36 inches tall, from left, depict a Mountain Man and two Santas.* Below: *The skills of business partners and designers Kale Bassler, left, and Terrie Wharton, right, complement each other.*

when Terrie's family built a new home, the two moved their growing operation to the home's lower level. This year they moved to a warehouse space in Coeur d'Alene at the back of a shop called Christmas at the Lake, operated by Gregg and Mary Peak. "It's fun for the customers in the shop to wander back to see artists at work," Kale says.

She says she never tires of Santa. "We pride ourselves in making one-of-a-kind Santas, and that's not as hard to do as you might think. There is no way we could make the same face twice. It just couldn't happen. Each one is different."

Making Santas has provided solace for the two artists. Kale has fought cancer twice. "If you can make yourself get up and do what you enjoy each day, it will help you get stronger."

THE BUSINESS SIDE

Terrie knows that too. She had a personal upset in her life about the time the two decided to try to start sculpting faces. "I sat there for hours, determined to teach myself how to sculpt. It helped take my mind off other matters. I think I made six faces before I stopped."

Just as they were determined to teach themselves artistic techniques, they were also resolved to make their business work right. Terrie picked the brains of colleagues in the corporate supermarket business. "Many times it doesn't matter if you are selling potatoes or Santa Claus figures. Some of the same principles apply. We also got lots of free information and help from the Small Business Administration in Spokane. Plus, we went over our plan with members of Senior Corps of Retired Executives, who were most helpful in pricing and working efficiently."

Santa checks the naughty and nice list and samples some holiday cookies at the same time.

Opposite, above: *A boy elf, dressed in festive holiday colors, has a twinkle in his eyes. He's about 22 inches tall. Opposite, below: Each elf has it's own impish look. Above: Elves take a break from their holiday activities. The girl in front, holding skates, is said to be the "sassy" one of the bunch, say her makers.*

The two now work about nine hours a day, six days a week, especially before big shows. When Christmas comes, they are exhausted. "I always think a cruise sounds good," Kale says.

"I'm always shocked that the towns are already decked out for the holidays," Terrie says. "I just want to spend time with my family."

But like Santa, they must gear up again soon. The first trade shows start in January.

The two giggle when they talk about Santa. They often say, "This is the best Santa I have ever made."

That's until the next one comes along.

Left: *These Santas deck the hall and the stairs with a jolly spirit.*
Below: *Like magic, Kale transforms clay into a sculpted face.*

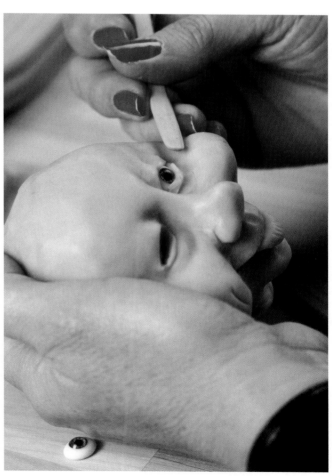

Show your love of Santa
with clay, paper, paint, and fabric
creations. These treasures
will bring holiday cheer for years
to come.

PERSONAL EXPRESSIONS

St. Nick Stocking

Constructed from felt and embellished with embroidery floss stitches, this St. Nick stocking is sure to be a holiday favorite.

What You'll Need

Tracing paper; pencil; scissors; ruler
½ yard of 45-inch-wide cream felt
5×11-inch piece of hunter green felt
3½×8-inch piece of cranberry red felt
5×6-inch piece of ivory felt; 2×2½-inch piece of tan felt
Paperback iron-on adhesive
5-inch square of cranberry red print fabric
5-inch square of blue and black print fabric; straight pins
Cotton embroidery floss in dark brown, ivory, and red
Embroidery needle; three ½-inch diameter ivory buttons
Two ⅝-inch diameter brown buttons

Here's How

1. Trace one full stocking and each individual piece from pattern, *pages 130–131*, onto tracing paper. Cut two stockings from cream felt. Cut heel and top border from green felt; cut scallop border and hearts from red felt; cut beard, mustache, and brim from ivory felt; and cut face from tan felt. In addition cut a 1½×1-inch tassel strip from ivory felt.

2. Draw around circle, hat, and toe patterns onto paper side of iron-on adhesive. Reverse hat and toe patterns to allow for proper direction after fusing. Following the manufacturer's instructions, fuse double-sided adhesive to backs of blue with black print and red print fabrics. Cut out pieces.

3. Remove paper backing from circle, hat, and toe pieces. Referring to stocking pattern, center circle 2½ inches below stocking top; fuse. Fuse toe piece over toe of stocking and hat in place on top of circle.

4. Pin face, beard, and then hat trim in place. Using two plies of red embroidery floss and blanket stitches, sew

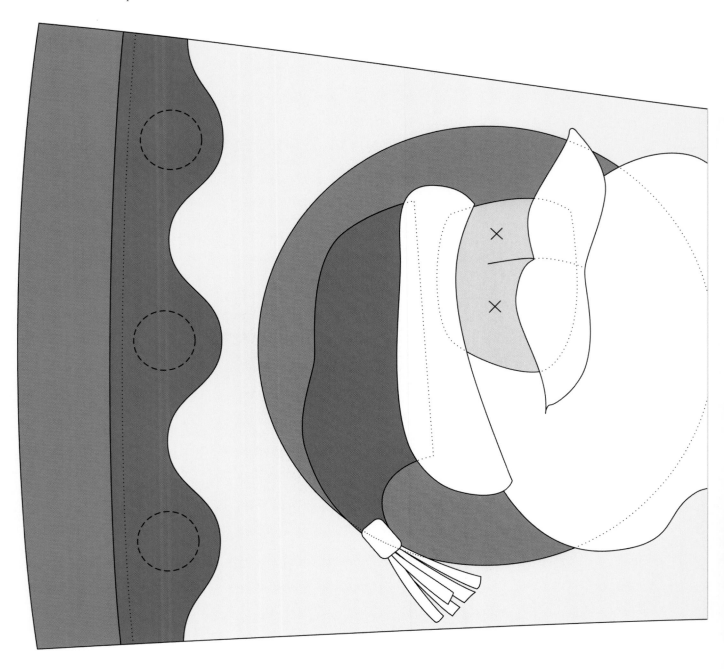

the brim to the stocking, spacing stitches ³⁄₁₆ inches apart. Use brown floss and buttonhole stitches to secure the outside edge of the beard and the edge to the left of the face. Also using brown floss, work eyes with large cross-stitches; backstitch the nose.

5. Attach mustache with ivory floss running stitch through vertical center.

6. For tassel cut ⅛-inch-wide fringe 1 inch deep across one long edge of tassel strip. Roll strip and wrap with ivory floss ¼ inch down from uncut rolled edge. Tack tassel to the tip of the hat.

7. Pin top border and scallop border in place, allowing scallop border to overlap bottom of top border. Using two strands of brown floss, sew along sides and tops of

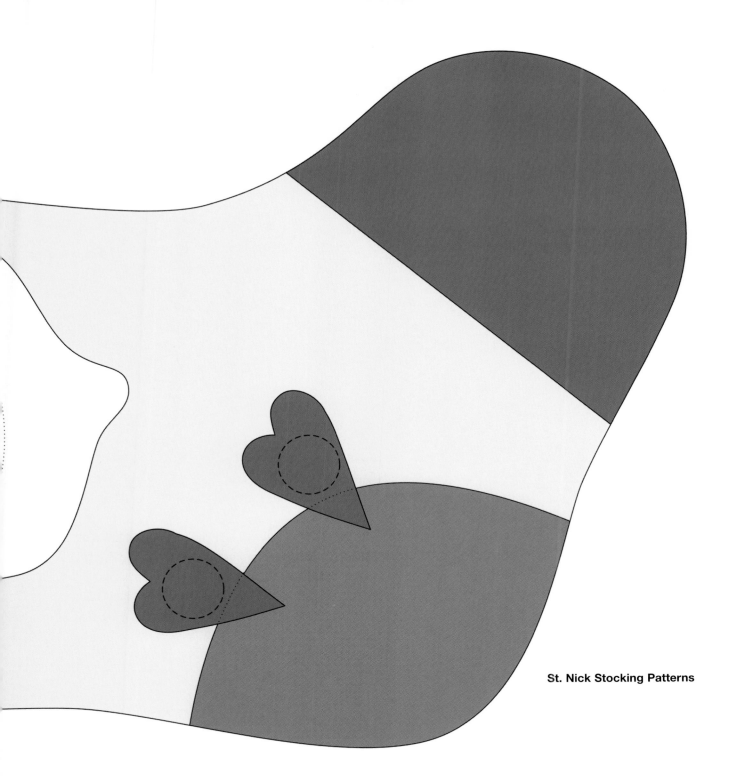

St. Nick Stocking Patterns

both borders using running stitches. Using ivory floss, sew ivory button to each scallop at dot.

8. Work large cross-stitches along top edge of toe piece using two plies of brown floss. Stitch heel piece in place. Tack hearts in place using brown buttons sewn with brown floss.

9. Cut two 12×¼-inch strips from green felt and one 12×¼-inch strip from red felt. Braid strips to make hanging loop. Fold strip in half, stack ends, and tack to back side of stocking front at outer top corner. Pin the stocking front to back, wrong sides facing. Using buttonhole stitch and two plies of brown floss, sew front to back, securing hanging loop.

Charming St. Nick

Curls of clay make this Santa seem happy from the top of his hat to the tip of his beard. Use oven-bake clay to create this clever fellow.

What You'll Need

Oven-bake clay, such as Sculpey, in beige, white,
    dark red, green, and black
Glass baking dish with flat bottom
Paper clip; ¼-inch-wide ribbon
Scissors; ruler

Here's How

1. Make a golf ball-size piece of beige clay. Shape into an oval and flatten until the shape is approximately ½ inch thick. Place the oval on a baking dish.

2. For nose roll two pea-size beige balls and one slightly larger ball. Press a smaller ball on each side of the larger one. Press the nose in the center of the oval.

3. Make half a golf ball-size piece of red clay. Shape into a ½-inch-thick triangle. Pull and shape one triangle point to form the hat's tip. Bend the tip slightly to the left. Place the hat on one end of the oval and press together.

4. For the hat brim roll a piece of white clay into a 3-inch-long cylinder, approximately the diameter of a pencil. Roll the ends into points. Shape the piece into an arch. Shape each end into a small coil. Press the shape firmly over the area where the hat meets the oval.

5. Make a large white coil for the tip of the hat. Make small white coils for the beard, mustache, and eyebrows, noting the shapes for each in the photograph, *left*. Make three small green coils for the hat embellishments. Press coils in place.

6. For eyes roll two tiny black ovals. Press into place just above the nose.

7. Bend a U-shape piece from a paper clip. Push the ends into the top of the hat, leaving a small loop for the hanger.

8. Bake the ornament in the oven according to the clay manufacturer's instructions. Let cool. Thread an 8-inch piece of ribbon through the paper clip loop. Tie the ribbon ends into a bow. Trim the ribbon ends.

Santa Sack Pattern 1 square = 1 inch

Santa Sack

As a fun lunch companion or a country-style gift wrap, this merry sack is sure to please even the most discriminating St. Nick.

What You'll Need

Tracing paper; pencil

Paper-back fusible web; scissors

Fabric scraps in red and white

Brown paper lunch sack

Paint pens in shiny white, shiny black, and
   iridescent glitter

Here's How

1. Enlarge and trace patterns, *above,* onto tracing paper. The dashed lines indicate the overlap. Mark the right side of each pattern piece.

2. Turn patterns, right side down, on paper side of fusible web and trace around the patterns. Cut out pieces ¼ inch outside the lines; fuse to wrong side of fabric.

3. Cut out on traced lines; peel off paper. Position pieces on bag and fuse in place.

4. Draw squiggly eyebrows with shiny white, make dot eyes with shiny black, and outline hat and beard with iridescent glitter "stitch" lines. Let dry.

Santa Doorstop

Greet holiday visitors with a handsome painted Santa that stands just over 10 inches tall.

What You'll Need

Tracing paper; pencil; scissors

¼ yard of navy blue fabric with gold snowflake print, or similar blue holiday print

8×12-inch piece of muslin; iron

8×12-inch piece of freezer paper; gesso

Fine grit sandpaper; tack cloth

Carbon paper; ballpoint pen

Acrylic paints, such as Delta Ceramcoat, in grape, metallic gold, navy blue, leaf green, wild rose, desert sun, medium flesh, black, denim blue, lichen gray, hammered iron, sandstone, magnolia white, yellow, blue jay, and mocha

Artist's paintbrushes; exterior varnish

Navy blue sewing thread

Polyester fiberfill; polyfil pellet beads; small funnel

32 inches of ⅛-inch diameter metallic gold cord

Hot-glue gun; glue sticks

Here's How

1. Trace base pattern and doorstop outline, *page 136*, onto tracing paper and cut out. Cut base and back piece from blue and gold print. Lay muslin rectangle atop shiny side of freezer paper. Using medium heat, iron fabric to paper. Let cool.

2. Apply a thin coat of gesso to fabric. Allow gesso to dry. Sand over gesso lightly in one direction; wipe with tack cloth. Apply second thin coat of gesso, sand, and wipe with tack cloth. Place carbon paper between pattern and doorstop front; transfer front piece outline and Santa, excluding face detail, by tracing over lines with ballpoint pen. Do not cut out doorstop front until all painting is completed.

3. Paint background grape. Add snowflakes and dots at random using metallic gold. Paint Santa's face medium flesh; let dry. Using pattern and carbon paper, transfer face detail. Shade nose and eyelids with desert sun. Blend wild rose into cheeks and tip of nose. Paint irises denim blue with black pupils. Dot inner corner of each eye with wild rose. Outline the eyes and nose with black.

4. Paint coat and hat denim blue with navy blue shading. Paint mittens blue jay; shade with denim blue. When mittens are dry, dot with gold.

5. Paint pants, star buttons, hat cuff, sleeve cuffs, collar, and star on hat yellow. Add navy blue checks to cuffs and collar, following pattern. Shade paints with mocha and add thin navy blue stripes when dry. Paint star button thread lines black.

6. Paint boots black; highlight with lichen gray. Paint beard, mustache, and eyebrows lichen gray; shade with hammered iron. First using sandstone and then magnolia white, paint thin lines to detail all hair. Paint holly leaves green and berries wild rose. Using a fine brush, outline clothing detail and holly leaves in black. Highlight eyes, tip of nose, all stars, boots, and holly berries with magnolia white. Let dry.

7. Apply a coat of varnish to painted doorstop front; let dry. Cut out front along cutting line.

8. Sew doorstop front to back using ⅛-inch seam allowance. Leave an opening for turning. Sew base to bottom; clip curves. Turn doorstop right side out and stuff top ¾ of figure firmly with polyester fiberfill.

9. Pour polyfil pellet beads into the bottom, using a funnel if necessary. Slipstitch the opening closed. Hot-glue the gold cord over the seamed edges.

Base for
Santa Doorstop
Cut 1

Center

Center

Santa Doorstop Patterns

Santa Greetings

Any jolly fellow can make these cute-but-easy cards in the wink of an eye.

What You'll Need for the Buckle Card

5½×8½-inch piece of red card stock

10-inch length of 1-inch-wide black grosgrain ribbon

White crafts glue; scissors

1½×1¾-inch piece of black card stock

Fine gold glitter

Black marking pen

Here's How

1. Fold the red card stock in half. Glue the ribbon around the card making the ends of the ribbon reach the edges of the card. Trim if necessary.

2. Cut out a small rectangle from the center of the black card stock. Apply glue evenly to the front of buckle and sprinkle with glitter. Glue on top of the ribbon. Let dry.

3. Write desired message inside card.

What You'll Need for the Hat Card

Red card stock; scissors; ruler

White felt; white crafts glue

White glitter

Black marking pen

Here's How

1. From red card stock, cut a 5¼×4¼-inch rectangle and a right triangle with 4-inch sides.

2. From felt cut a 1×5¼-inch strip and a 1¼-inch circle.

3. Run a bead of glue along the top of the red card stock rectangle. Lay the triangle on the glue, leaving the bottom point open.

4. Glue the felt strip to the bottom of the rectangle. Glue the circle to the point of the triangle.

5. Spread glue on the felt circle and strip; dust with glitter. Write desired message under the hat flap.

SWEET SENSATIONS

Let your love of Santa carry through to your holiday baking. This festive collection of cookie and cake recipes inspires you to make unforgettable treats for your family and friends at Christmastime.

Opposite: *Gingerbread dough is cut into teardrop shapes to make Santa and his helpers.*

Santa Delights

WELCOME SANTA INTO THE KITCHEN WITH
SENSATIONAL TREATS TO TEMPT BELIEVERS OF ALL AGES.

Gingerbread Cutouts

Read Cutting and Baking on page 142 *before beginning.*

½ cup shortening

½ cup sugar

1 teaspoon baking powder

1 teaspoon ground ginger

½ teaspoon baking soda

½ teaspoon ground cinnamon

½ teaspoon ground cloves

½ cup molasses

1 egg

1 tablespoon vinegar

2½ cups all-purpose flour

1 recipe Royal Icing *(page 142)*

1. In a bowl beat shortening with an electric mixer on medium to high speed 30 seconds. Add sugar, baking powder, ginger, baking soda, cinnamon, and cloves. Beat until combined, scraping sides of bowl occasionally.

Beat in the molasses, egg, and vinegar until combined. Beat in as much of the flour as you can with the mixer. Stir in remaining flour. Divide dough in half. Cover and chill for 3 hours or until easy to handle.

2. Follow the Cutting and Baking Instructions, *below*, to complete the gingerbread cutouts.

Royal Icing: *Make icing just before needed for decorating and assembling.* In a large bowl combine 3 tablespoons meringue powder*, ½ cup warm water, 1 sifted 16-ounce package powdered sugar (4½ cups), 1 teaspoon vanilla, and ½ teaspoon cream of tartar. Beat with an electric mixer on low speed until combined; beat on high speed for 7 to 10 minutes or until very stiff. Makes about 5 cups. **Note: Look for meringue powder at kitchen, cake-decorating, and crafts shops.*

Cutting and Baking

1. Use tracing paper and a pencil to copy the patterns, *opposite.* Use patterns to cut shapes from thin cardboard. Cover them with clear adhesive plastic to protect them.

2. On a lightly floured surface, using a lightly floured rolling pin, roll out about half of Gingerbread Cutouts Dough to ⅛ inch thick. Place pattern pieces on top of dough and cut around pattern pieces with a sharp knife. Reroll scraps, if necessary, to get four chimney sides and four chimney tops. Using the tip of a table knife, lightly score the chimney pieces in a brick pattern (see photo, *top right*). Roll out remaining dough and cut out Santa and reindeer using 3- to 4-inch cookie cutters.

3. With a large spatula transfer gingerbread dough pieces to a cookie sheet, leaving 1 inch between pieces.

4. Bake in a 375° oven for 6 to 8 minutes or longer for cookies and 7 to 9 minutes or longer for larger pieces, until centers are just firm. Place patterns over the hot chimney cutouts. Carefully retrim edges. Return cookie sheet to

Above top: *Use a table knife to press a brick pattern in gingerbread.*

Above: *Use a paintbrush to paint red icing on brick sections.*

oven and bake for 2 to 3 minutes more or until very firm. Cool slightly; transfer to wire rack to cool completely.

Decorating

Note: You will need a small amount of red and black icing "paint" to decorate Santa and chimney and some white and red icing for piping. Keep all icings covered with plastic wrap until ready to use them.

1. Prepare the Royal Icing using the recipe, *left.* Place about 1 cup of icing in a small bowl. Tint icing with red gel paste food coloring. Place about half of the red icing in another small bowl. Add just enough water until icing is about the consistency of corn syrup. Place the thicker red icing in a decorating bag fitted with a coupler and small round tip. Place about 2 tablespoons prepared Royal Icing in a small bowl; tint with black gel

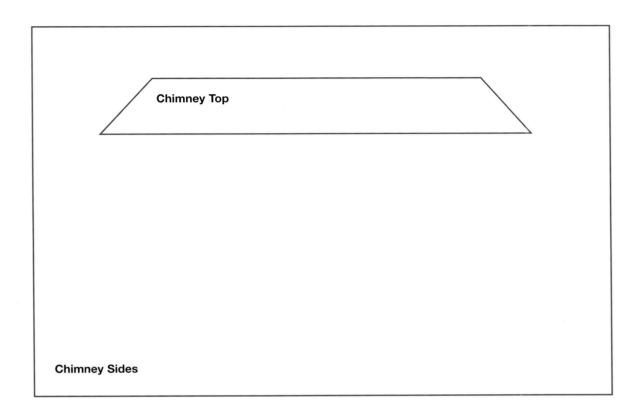

Chimney Top

Chimney Sides

paste food coloring. Add just enough water until icing is also the consistency of corn syrup. Place about half of the remaining prepared Royal Icing in a decorating bag fitted with a coupler and a small star tip. The final remaining prepared Royal Icing will be used for making icicles. It should be thinned with just enough water until the consistency of cake batter.

2. Using a tiny artist's brush and the red icing, paint Santa's hat, coat, pants, and all the chimney bricks. (See bottom photo, *opposite.*) Let pieces dry. Meanwhile use the black icing to paint Santa's mittens, boots, and belt. Use the white icing in the decorating bag to add Santa's beard, coat and hat trim, mustache, and eyebrows. Use the red icing in a decorating bag to pipe reins on reindeer. Add a few silver dragées as sleigh bells if desired. Let dry.

Assembly

1. To assemble the chimney, pipe a line of white icing along the edge of a chimney piece. Press another

chimney edge into the wet line of icing. Use soup cans to hold chimney pieces in place until set. Repeat with a line of icing at each corner. When icing is set, about 30 minutes, remove soup cans. Attach the chimney top pieces with a thick line of white icing at top edge of the four chimney walls. Let assembled chimney dry for 1 to 2 hours before adding icicles. To create icicles spread a generous amount of thinned white icing on top of one chimney side. Allow some of icing to drip over edge. Repeat with remaining top sides, working on one side at a time. If desired, while icing is still wet, sprinkle with some fine sanding sugar or granulated sugar. Let dry.

2. To assemble standing reindeer, attach small triangle gingerbread pieces to the back of them with piped icing.

Arranging

1. Fill the chimney half full with extra baked gingerbread cookies. Stand Santa on top of the cookies. Arrange reindeer around the chimney.

Chocolate Reindeer

Bake these adorable reindeer for a holiday-time treat.

1	cup butter, softened
1½	cups sugar
⅓	cup unsweetened cocoa powder
2	teaspoons cream of tartar
1	teaspoon baking soda
½	teaspoon salt
3	eggs
1	teaspoon vanilla
3¼	cups all-purpose flour
72	small pretzel twists
72	candy-coated milk chocolate pieces
36	small red gumdrops

1. In a large bowl beat butter with an electric mixer on medium to high speed for 30 seconds. Add sugar, cocoa powder, cream of tartar, baking soda, and salt. Beat until combined, scraping sides of bowl occasionally. Beat in eggs and vanilla until combined. Beat in as much of the flour as possible with the mixer. Using a wooden spoon, stir in remaining flour.

2. Divide dough into six equal portions. Wrap portions in waxed paper or plastic wrap. Chill for 3 hours.

3. On a lightly floured surface, roll each dough portion into a circle 6 inches in diameter. Using a knife, cut each circle into six wedges. Place wedges 2 inches apart on an ungreased cookie sheet.

4. For antlers, on each triangle lightly press a pretzel into each upper corner. Press in chocolate pieces for eyes. For a nose press a red gumdrop into the triangle.

5. Bake in a 375° oven for 7 to 9 minutes or until edges are firm. Do not overbake. Cool on cookie sheet for 1 minute; transfer to a wire rack; cool. Makes 36 cookies.

Clever Cut-Up Santa Cake

Bake round and square cakes to make this jolly fellow.

1   **package 2-layer-size white cake mix**
      Creamy White Frosting
      Red food coloring
1   **large marshmallow**
2   **blue candy-coated, chocolate-covered**
      peanuts, such as peanut M&M's
1   **red jaw breaker**
3   **red fruit-flavor circle candies, such as Life Savers**
      Flaked coconut
3–4 **candy-coated, fruit-flavored pieces, such as Skittles**

1. Prepare cake mix according to the package directions, using 1 greased and floured 8-inch round baking pan and 1 greased and floured 8×8×2-inch baking pan. Let cool in pans on wire rack for 10 minutes. Remove from pans and cool completely. If necessary, trim tops of cakes so that both cakes are the same height.

2. To shape Santa, cut off about one-third of the round cake. Place the larger piece on serving platter or a large piece of cardboard covered with foil. Place the flat side of cake facing up. (This will be Santa's head.) Place the smaller piece under the larger piece with the curved edge touching the larger piece. (This will be Santa's shoulders.) Cut a 1-inch strip of cake off of one side of the square cake. (This will be the bottom of Santa's hat.) Place at the top of Santa's head.

3. Cut the remaining piece of cake into two triangles. For the hat, place one of the triangles with the longer side touching the 1-inch piece at the top of the head. Place the remaining triangle at an angle, fitting it against the other triangle.

4. Tint ½ cup of the Creamy White Frosting to desired color pink for face, using the red food coloring. Tint 1¼ cups of the frosting to desired red color for hat and shoulders. Leave remaining frosting white.

5. Frost face, hat, and shoulders with appropriate colors of frosting. Using a small star tip, pipe white frosting onto the brim of Santa's hat. Place marshmallow at the tip of the hat. Add eyes using blue candy-coated, chocolate-covered peanuts. Use a red jaw breaker for a nose and red fruit-flavor circle candy for mouth and cheeks. Secure to face with some of the white frosting. Pipe on a beard, mustache, and eyebrows. Sprinkle beard with coconut. Add candy-coated, fruit-flavor pieces to front of Santa's shirt for buttons.

Creamy White Frosting: Beat 1 cup shortening, 1½ teaspoons vanilla, and ½ teaspoon almond extract with an electric mixer until combined. Slowly add 2¼ cups sifted powdered sugar, beating well. Add 2 tablespoons milk. Gradually beat in 2¼ cups more sifted powdered sugar and enough milk to make spreading consistency. Makes 3 cups.

Toy Cookies

For kids the only thing better than getting their heart's desire in a stocking is getting it with a glass of milk before bed. Shape these cookies into your (or your child's) favorite kind of toy.

¾   **cup butter, softened**
⅔   **cup butter-flavor or regular shortening**
1½ **cups sugar**
1   **tablespoon baking powder**
¼   **teaspoon salt**
2   **eggs**
2   **teaspoons vanilla**
4   **cups all-purpose flour**
    Paste or liquid food coloring

1. In bowl beat butter and shortening for 30 seconds. Add sugar, baking powder, and salt. Beat until combined. Beat in eggs and vanilla until combined. Beat in as much of the flour with the mixer as you can. Stir in any remaining flour (dough should be stiff).

2. Divide dough into portions, one for each color to be used. Knead food coloring into each portion, adding it slowly until desired color is obtained. Cover and chill for 2 to 24 hours. Shape dough into toy shapes (as described, *below,* or others). Place cookies 2 inches apart on an ungreased cookie sheet.

3. Bake in a 300° oven for 18 to 20 minutes or until edges are firm. Carefully transfer cookies to a wire rack; cool. Makes about 40 cookies.

Car/Bus: Flatten a 1½-inch piece of dough into a triangle with 2-inch sides. Round the corners and gently press the sides to make a vehicle body. Add two ½-inch balls for wheels. If desired, flatten pieces of dough for windows, headlights, bumpers, and people inside (see photo, *right*).

Tractor: For large wheel flatten a 1¼-inch ball of dough. For tractor body flatten a 1-inch ball of dough; attach to large wheel. For small wheel flatten a ¾-inch ball of dough. For cab shape a ¾-inch ball of dough; attach to large wheel and tractor body. For engine and hubcap shape ½-inch balls of dough.

Teddy Bear: For body flatten a 1½-inch ball of dough to about 1½ inches across. For head flatten a ¾-inch ball of dough to about 1 inch across; press in place. Make six ⅜-inch balls; press in place for ears, arms, and legs. Add small dots of dough for eyes, nose, and mouth.

Boat: For the base flatten a 1½-inch ball of dough into an oval about 2½ inches across; curve ends up slightly. For a mast attach a 2-inch-long piece of a different color in the center top of the base. For sails flatten two triangles of dough and attach to mast.

Visions-of-Sugarplums Pizza

These bejeweled treats send little ones to sweet dreams. A hint: Smaller gumdrops usually are spicy, and larger ones usually are not. If you prefer, substitute jelly beans or other small candies.

⅔   **cup butter, softened**
¾   **cup sugar**
1   **teaspoon ground ginger**
½   **teaspoon baking soda**
½   **teaspoon ground cinnamon**
1   **egg**
2   **tablespoons molasses**
1¾   **cups all-purpose flour**
1¾   **cups halved small and/or sliced large gumdrops**
½   **cup white baking pieces**
1½   **teaspoons butter-flavor or regular shortening**

1. Lightly grease a 12- or 13-inch pizza pan or a 13×9×2-inch baking pan; set aside.

2. In a large mixing bowl beat butter with an electric mixer on medium to high speed for 30 seconds. Add sugar, ginger, baking soda, and cinnamon. Beat until combined, scraping sides of bowl occasionally. Beat in egg and molasses until combined. Beat in as much of the flour as possible with the mixer. Using a wooden spoon, stir in any remaining flour.

3. Spread the dough evenly into the prepared pan.

4. Bake in a 350° oven for 12 minutes. Sprinkle partially baked cookie with gumdrops. Return to oven. Bake about 8 minutes more or until edges are browned (avoid overbaking). Cool completely in pan on a wire rack.

5. In a heavy, small saucepan, melt white baking pieces and shortening over low heat. Drizzle over cookie. Let stand about 20 to 30 minutes or until set. To serve cut into wedges or bars. Makes 16 wedges.

Santa Madeleines

These soft, cakey little cookies from France are made sweeter still when formed into the cherry-cheeked likeness of the jolliest old elf of them all—Santa Claus.

¾ cup all-purpose flour

¼ teaspoon baking powder

1 egg

2 egg yolks

1 cup sifted powdered sugar

½ cup butter, melted and cooled

2 teaspoons finely shredded orange peel

2 teaspoons orange juice

½ teaspoon anise seed, crushed (optional)

1 recipe Decorator Frosting or 2 cans vanilla frosting
   Red, pink, green, black and/or blue paste
     food coloring
   Small round candies (optional)

1. Grease and flour twenty-four 3-inch Madeleine molds; set aside. Stir together flour and baking powder; set aside.

2. In a medium mixing bowl, beat egg and egg yolks with an electric mixer on high speed 5 minutes or until thick and lemon-colored. Add powdered sugar; beat on low speed until combined and then on high speed about 5 minutes more or until very thick and satiny. Beat in butter with an electric mixer on low speed. Add flour mixture, beating on low speed until combined. Stir in orange peel, orange juice, and, if using, anise seed. Carefully spoon batter into the prepared molds, filling each three-fourths full.

3. Bake in a 375° oven about 10 minutes or until edges are golden and tops spring back. Cool in molds on rack 1 minute. Loosen cookies with a knife. Invert cookies onto a rack and cool completely.

4. Divide frosting, leaving about half of it white; color one-third with red and/or pink food coloring and remaining with green, black, and/or blue food coloring.

5. To decorate, fill a decorating bag fitted with a small star tip with white frosting. Pipe on hat trim at an angle about a third of the way down from narrow end of cookie. Fill decorating bag fitted with a small star or plain tip with red or pink frosting; pipe on hat. With white frosting, pipe on mustache, beard, and pom-pom on hat. Fill decorating bag fitted with a small round tip with green, black, or blue frosting; pipe on eyes. Using red frosting, pipe on mouth. Pipe on other frosting decorations. (Or use small round candies for eyes, nose, mouth, and cheeks, attaching them with frosting.) Wrap cookies tightly to store. Makes 24 cookies.

Decorator Frosting: Beat 1 cup shortening and 1½ teaspoons vanilla on medium speed for 30 seconds. Slowly add 2 cups sifted powdered sugar; beat well. Beat in 2 tablespoons milk. Gradually beat in 2½ cups sifted powdered sugar and enough milk to make piping consistency.

Santa's Lists

Santa (or someone with more permanent residence at your house) may make these lists, but he won't have a chance to check them twice if hungry elves are around!

1	cup butter, softened
½	of an 8-ounce can almond paste (½ cup)
1	cup sugar
1	teaspoon baking powder
1	egg
1	tablespoon finely shredded orange peel
3	cups all-purpose flour
	Powdered food coloring
1	recipe Decorating Icing (optional)

1. In a large mixing bowl, beat butter and almond paste with an electric mixer on medium to high speed for 30 seconds. Add sugar and baking powder. Beat until combined, scraping sides of bowl occasionally. Beat in egg and orange peel until combined. Beat in as much of the flour as possible with the mixer. Using a wooden spoon, stir in remaining flour.

2. Pack unchilled dough into a cookie press fitted with a ribbon plate. Force dough through press onto an ungreased cookie sheet in the shape of a curved scroll (see photo, *left*), cutting into desired lengths.

3. Bake in a 375° oven for 5 to 6 minutes or until edges of cookies are firm but not brown. Transfer cookies to a wire rack; cool. When cooled, if desired, brush cookies with powdered food coloring and use Decorating Icing in a decorating bag with a writing tip to spell out names on cookies. Makes about 80 cookies.

Decorating Icing: In a small mixing bowl combine 3 cups sifted powdered sugar and enough milk (3 to 5 tablespoons) to make an icing of piping consistency. If desired, stir in a few drops of food coloring.

Elf Hats

To give these meringue elf toppers their jocular colored pom-poms, pipe on a bit of tinted icing after baking.

2	egg whites
½	teaspoon vanilla
⅛	teaspoon cream of tartar
	Few drops green or red food coloring
⅔	cup sugar
6	ounces bittersweet chocolate or semisweet chocolate, melted
¾	cup finely chopped walnuts
	Purchased decorating icing (optional)

1. In a medium mixing bowl allow egg whites to stand at room temperature for 30 minutes. Meanwhile grease a cookie sheet; set aside.

2. For meringue add vanilla, cream of tartar, and food coloring to the egg whites. Beat with an electric mixer on medium speed until soft peaks form (tips curl). Gradually add sugar, 1 tablespoon at a time, beating about 5 minutes on high speed until stiff peaks form (tips stand straight).

3. Spoon meringue into pastry bag fitted with ½-inch round tip. Pipe small 1-inch-high mounds that end in an angled tip about 1 inch apart on prepared sheet.

4. Bake in a 300° oven about 15 minutes or until edges are very lightly browned. Transfer cookies to a wire rack; cool.

5. When cookies are cool, dip bottoms into melted chocolate and then into chopped walnuts. Set on waxed paper until chocolate is firm. If desired add a dot of colored icing to each tip. Makes about 48 cookies.

Peppermint Candy Canes

Make these delightful cookie canes with either red- or green-tinted dough or combine the two colors in one cane.

⅓   cup butter, softened
⅓   cup shortening
¾   cup sugar
1   teaspoon baking powder
     Dash salt
1   egg
1   tablespoon milk
½   teaspoon vanilla
½   teaspoon peppermint extract
2   cups all-purpose flour
     Red or green paste food coloring
     Sugar (optional)

1. In a medium mixing bowl beat butter and shortening with an electric mixer on medium to high speed for 30 seconds. Add the ¾ cup sugar, baking powder, and salt. Beat until combined, scraping sides of bowl occasionally. Beat in egg, milk, vanilla, and peppermint extract. Beat in as much of the flour as possible with the mixer. Using a wooden spoon, stir in any remaining flour.

2. Divide dough in half. Stir red or green paste food coloring into half of the dough. If necessary cover and chill dough for 30 to 60 minutes or until dough is easy to handle.

3. Divide each half into six pieces. Roll each piece into a 12-inch-long rope. Lay ropes side by side on a lightly floured surface, alternating colors. Use a rolling pin to flatten assembled ropes into about a 14×9-inch rectangle that is ¼ inch thick. Using a pastry cutter, pizza wheel, or long sharp knife, cut the rectangle diagonally into ½-inch-wide strips. Cut strips into pieces 5 to 7 inches long. (Press shorter strips together end to end to reach desired length.) Place on an ungreased cookie sheet. Curve one end of each piece to form a candy cane. If desired sprinkle lightly with additional sugar.

4. Bake in a 375° oven for 7 to 8 minutes or until edges are firm and bottoms are very lightly browned. Transfer cookies to a wire rack; cool. Makes about 36 cookies.

Pealing Bells

These buttery Christmas bells may be soundless, but they delight your senses of sight and taste.

1	cup butter, softened
1	cup granulated sugar
2	tablespoons milk
1	teaspoon vanilla
2½	cups all-purpose flour
½	cup colored sugar or nonpareils (optional)
30	maraschino cherries, halved and well drained, or small candies

1. In a large mixing bowl beat butter with an electric mixer on medium to high speed for 30 seconds. Add granulated sugar. Beat until combined, scraping sides of bowl occasionally. Beat in milk and vanilla until combined. Beat in as much of the flour as possible. Using a wooden spoon, stir in any remaining flour.

2. Divide dough in half. Shape each half of dough into an 8-inch-long roll. If desired roll in colored sugar to coat. Wrap each roll in plastic wrap or waxed paper. Chill for 4 to 24 hours.

3. Using a sharp knife, cut dough into ¼-inch-thick slices. Place slices on an ungreased cookie sheet. Fold in sides of each slice, overlapping where they meet; pinch in sides to form a bell shape.

4. Bake in a 350° oven for 12 to 14 minutes or until edges are firm. Immediately press a cherry half at the bottom of each slice for a bell clapper. Transfer cookies to a wire rack; cool. Makes about 60 cookies.

Gingerbread Cutouts

Use this timeless cutout cookie recipe to make limitless Christmas images—Santa and his helpers, stars, reindeer, or scampering gingerbread kids.

2½ cups all-purpose flour

1   cup whole wheat flour

1   teaspoon ground cinnamon

1   teaspoon ground ginger

¾   teaspoon baking soda

½   teaspoon ground nutmeg

¼   teaspoon salt

¼   teaspoon ground cloves

1   cup butter, softened

1   cup sugar

1   egg

½   cup molasses

2   tablespoons lemon juice

1   recipe Royal Icing

    Food coloring

    Small candies for decorating

1. In a medium bowl stir together all-purpose and whole wheat flours, cinnamon, ginger, baking soda, nutmeg, salt, and cloves; set aside.

2. In a large mixing bowl, beat butter with an electric mixer on medium to high speed for 30 seconds. Add sugar; beat until fluffy. Beat in egg until mixture is light. Beat in molasses and lemon juice on low speed until combined. Beat in as much of flour mixture as possible with the mixer. Stir in any remaining flour mixture.

3. Divide dough in half. Cover and chill at least 3 hours or until dough is easy to handle.

4. On a lightly floured surface, roll half of the dough at a time to ⅛-inch thickness. Using cookie cutters, cut out dough. (For Santas use teardrop-shape cookie cutters of various sizes.) Place 1 inch apart on an ungreased cookie sheet.

5. Bake in a 350° oven for 8 to 10 minutes or until edges are lightly browned. Cool on cookie sheet for 1 minute. Transfer cookies to a wire rack; cool. When cookies are cool, decorate with white or tinted Royal Icing and candies. Makes about 90 (2½-inch) cookies.

Royal Icing: In a medium mixing bowl combine 2 cups sifted powdered sugar and 4 teaspoons meringue powder.* Add 3 tablespoons cold water. Beat with an electric mixer on low speed until mixture is combined; then beat on medium to high speed for 5 to 8 minutes or until mixture forms stiff peaks. (If mixture seems stiff while beating, add water ½ teaspoon at a time. Icing should be fairly thick for piping. For a thinner glazing consistency, stir in a little more water after beating.) When not using, keep icing tightly covered to prevent it from drying out; keep refrigerated. Makes 2 cups.

*Note: Look for meringue powder at kitchen, cake-decorating, and crafts shops.

1. In a large mixing bowl beat butter and shortening with an electric mixer on medium to high speed for 30 seconds. Add sugar, baking soda, and salt. Beat until combined, scraping sides of bowl occasionally. Beat in the egg, egg yolk, milk, and vanilla. Beat in as much of the flour as possible with the mixer. Using a wooden spoon, stir in any remaining flour.

2. Divide dough into three equal portions. Use it to make Santa's Whiskers, Chocolate-Mint Thumbprints, and Lemon-Almond Tea Cookies.

Santa's Whiskers

Everyone will love these polka-dot cherry treats complete with coconut "whiskers."

¾ **cup maraschino cherries, drained and finely chopped**
⅓ **recipe Trio Cookie Dough**
    Few drops red food coloring (optional)
½ **cup coconut**

1. Pat cherries dry with paper towels. In a medium bowl combine cherries, Trio Cookie Dough, and food coloring. Using a wooden spoon, mix until thoroughly combined.

2. Shape dough into a 10-inch-long roll. Roll dough in coconut until covered. Wrap in plastic wrap or waxed paper. Chill in the refrigerator for at least 4 hours or until firm.

3. Using a knife, cut dough into ¼-inch-thick slices. Place slices 2 inches apart on an ungreased cookie sheet.

4. Bake in a 375° oven for 8 to 10 minutes or until edges are firm and bottoms are lightly browned. Transfer cookies to a wire rack; cool. Makes about 36 cookies.

Trio Cookie Dough

When holiday time is tight, use one dough to create three cookies —Santa's Whiskers, Chocolate-Mint Thumbprints, and Lemon-Almond Tea Cookies.

¾   **cup butter, softened**
¾   **cup shortening**
1½ **cups sugar**
¼   **teaspoon baking soda**
¼   **teaspoon salt**
1   **egg**
1   **egg yolk**
3   **tablespoons milk**
1½ **teaspoons vanilla**
4½ **cups all-purpose flour**

Chocolate-Mint Thumbprints

A cooling, crisp-as-the-winter-air mint filling tops off these soft, rich, chocolate cookies.

⅓   **recipe Trio Cookie Dough**
2   **ounces semisweet chocolate, melted and cooled**
2   **teaspoons milk**
1   **recipe Peppermint Filling**
¼   **cup chopped candy canes or hard peppermint candies**

1. In a medium mixing bowl combine the cookie dough, chocolate, and milk. Mix until thoroughly combined.

2. Shape dough into an 8-inch-long roll. Wrap in plastic wrap or waxed paper. Chill in the refrigerator for at least 1 hour.

3. Using a sharp knife, cut dough into ¾-inch-thick slices. Cut each slice into quarters and roll each quarter into a ball. Place balls 2 inches apart on ungreased cookie sheet. Press down in center of each ball with your thumb.

4. Bake in a 375° oven for 8 to 10 minutes or until tops look dry. Transfer cookies to a wire rack; cool.

5. Spoon a scant teaspoon of Peppermint Filling into the center of each cookie. Sprinkle cookies with the chopped candy. Makes about 48 cookies.

Peppermint Filling: In a small mixing bowl beat ¼ cup butter with an electric mixer on medium speed about 30 seconds or until softened. Gradually add 1 cup sifted powered sugar, beating until combined. Beat in 2 tablespoons milk, ¼ teaspoon peppermint extract, and a few drops of red or green food coloring, if desired. Gradually beat in 1 cup sifted powdered sugar until smooth.

Lemon-Almond Tea Cookies

These elegant little cookies make perfect fare for a holiday open house.

⅓   **recipe Trio Cookie Dough**
2   **teaspoons finely shredded lemon peel**
1   **teaspoon almond extract**
1   **recipe Lemon Frosting**
½   **cup sliced almonds, toasted**

1. In a medium bowl combine the cookie dough, lemon peel, and almond extract. Using a wooden spoon, mix until thoroughly combined.

2. Shape dough into an 8-inch-long roll. Wrap in plastic wrap or waxed paper. Chill in the refrigerator for at least 4 hours.

3. Using a sharp knife, cut dough into ¼-inch-thick slices. Place slices 2 inches apart on an ungreased cookie sheet.

4. Bake in a 375° oven for 8 to 10 minutes or until edges are firm and bottoms are lightly browned. Transfer cookies to a wire rack; cool.

5. Spread about 1 teaspoon of the frosting on each cookie. Sprinkle with sliced almonds. Makes 32 cookies.

Lemon Frosting: In a small bowl beat ¼ cup softened butter with an electric mixer on medium to high speed about 30 seconds. Gradually add 1 cup sifted powdered sugar, beating until combined. Beat in 4 teaspoons milk, 1 teaspoon lemon juice, ¼ teaspoon vanilla, and a few drops almond extract. Gradually beat in 1 cup sifted powdered sugar until smooth.

Sources

CAROL FIELD DAHLSTROM *Editor*
cfdahlstrom@aol.com

————

SINTERKLAAS CELEBRATION *Pages 22–23*
Pella, IA 50219
www.pella.org

————

BARBARA AND HARRY BUDD *Pages 26–31, 50–55*
For information on a Christmas tour of their home:
www.Santahouse.org

————

BARBARA KISSINGER *Pages 56–63*
Burlington, IA 52601
319/752-0226
bakissinger@lisco.com

————

LAURA BENGE *Pages 72–77*
Rudd, IA 50471
641/395-2682
cowpie@omnitelcom.com

————

SUSAN EWING *Pages 78–85*
Highland, UT 84003
801/763-9566
www.susanewingoriginals.com

————

LEO SMITH FOLK ART *Pages 86–95*
Fountain City, WI 54629
608/687-6698
www.leosmith.com

————

TERI EMBREY *Pages 102–109*
Santas for the Soul
206/242-4453
www.teriembrey.com

————

SUE CORNELISON *Pages 110–115*
St. Charles, IA 50240
641/396-2290

————

NORTHWEST SANTA CREATIONS *Pages 116–125*
Kale Bassler and Terrie Wharton
517 E. Sherman Ave.
Coeur d'Alene, ID 83814
800/261-3661
208/765-1077
www.NorthwestSantaCreations.com

————

ST. NICK STOCKING *Pages 128–131*
Felt—National Nonwovens
P.O. Box 150
Easthampton, MA 01027

————

CHARMING ST. NICK *Page 132*
Polymer Clay—Sculpey
Polyform Products Co.
1901 Estes Avenue
Elk Grove Village, IL 60007
www.scupley.com

————

SANTA DOORSTOP *Pages 134–136*
Paint—Delta Ceramcoat
Delta Technicl Coatings, Inc.
2550 Pellissier Place
Whittier, CA 90601-1505
800/423-4135

————

SANTA GREETINGS *Page 137*
Card Stock—DMD, Inc.
800/805-9890

————

SANTA MADELEINES *Pages 148–149*
Madeleine Pan—Sweet Celebrations
800/328-6722
www.sweetc.com

Better Homes and Gardens®

Santa Claus

C O L L E C T I O N

Editor:	Carol Field Dahlstrom
Writers:	Chris Ellibee, Carol McGarvey
Graphic Designer:	Sue Ellibee
Technical Editor:	Susan M. Banker
Contributing Producers:	Nicole Lozier, Trish Maharam
Contributing Technical Assistant:	Judy Bailey
Copy Chief:	Terri Fredrickson
Publishing Operations Manager:	Karen Schirm
Managers, Book Production:	Pam Kvitne, Marjorie J. Schenkelberg, Rick von Holdt, Mark Weaver
Edit and Design Production Coordinator:	Mary Lee Gavin
Contributing Copy Editor:	Arianna McKinney
Contributing Proofreaders:	Karen Grossman, Beth Havey, Sara Henderson
Photographers:	John Reed Foresman, Mike Jensen, Scott Little, Andy Lyons Cameraworks, Stuart Ruckman
Photostyling Assistant:	Donna Chesnut
Technical Illustrator:	Chris Neubauer Graphics, Inc.
Editorial Assistants:	Kaye Chabot, Cheryl Eckert
Scout:	Jean Thomas
Food Artist:	Jennifer Petersen

MEREDITH® BOOKS

Editor in Chief:	Linda Raglan Cunningham
Design Director:	Matt Strelecki
Executive Editor:	Jennifer Dorland Darling
Managing Editor:	Gregory H. Kayko

Publisher:	James D. Blume
Executive Director, Marketing:	Jeffrey Myers
Executive Director, New Business Development:	Todd M. Davis
Executive Director, Sales:	Ken Zagor
Director, Operations:	George A. Susral
Director, Production:	Douglas M. Johnston
Business Director:	Jim Leonard

Vice President and General Manager:	Douglas J. Guendel

BETTER HOMES AND GARDENS® MAGAZINE

Editor in Chief:	Karol DeWulf Nickell

MEREDITH PUBLISHING GROUP

President, Publishing Group:	Stephen M. Lacy
Vice President-Publishing Director:	Bob Mate

MEREDITH CORPORATION

Chairman and Chief Executive Officer:	William T. Kerr

Merry Christmas
to all and to all a
good night!